FLIRT*coach*

Communication Tips for Friendship, Love
and Professional Success

Peta Heskell

element

Element
An Imprint of HarperCollins*Publishers*
77–85 Fulham Palace Road
Hammersmith, London W6 8JB

The Element website is: www.elementbooks.co.uk

element ™

and *Element*
are trademarks of
HarperCollins*Publishers* Limited

First published by Thorsons, an Imprint of HarperCollins*Publishers* 2001
This edition published by Element 2002

13 12 11 10 9 8 7 6

A catalogue record for this book
is available from the British Library

ISBN 0 00 710843 5

Printed and bound in Great Britain by
Martins the Printers Limited, Berwick upon Tweed

This book is dedicated to Billy Kerr. Billy, because you know what it means to live life positively, being who you are and approaching every day with a smile on your face and hope for the future. That's why you found your soulmate!

CONTENTS

ACKNOWLEDGEMENTS

Sometimes when you take a leap into the adventure of your life there are master teachers who appear at just the right time. Two such people came into my life and it has never been the same since – for which I am eternally grateful.

Joseph Riggio

Joseph, you have been a true mentor, friend and teacher to me. Your integrity and openness, 'sense-ability', playfulness, strength and way of being in the world have touched me and expanded my life beyond what I thought possible. You taught me how to be 'me at my best'. At times, like any good mentor, you have occasionally rapped me severely over the knuckles and no doubt will continue to do so, and I thank you for that. You're a pip!

Richard Bandler

The king of explorers, Richard has spent his life jumping into the abyss of the unknown, trying out wild and seemingly crazy ways of managing his brain and body, and Richard, you have passed all that along to me in your superbly crafted, energetic, illuminating and hilarious trainings. The sound of your voice still rings in my ears. But more than that, Richard, you have infused me with thoughts of the most exciting kind. Thanks for the divinely devilish inspiration.

I'd also like to thank Lesley, a true SuccessFlirt. Lesley has been my friend and confidante for many years and her way of living is a delight as well as a source of inspiration for this book.

And Jeff, thanks for allowing me to share your infectious enthusiam for life.

My parents, John and Shelagh, who apart from loving and cherishing me as a child, also took care of all my tedious domestic chores while I wrote this book. I love you.

A very special thanks to Ken for 15 years of support, love and encouragement.

Thank you to all the people who attended my flirting weekends for being brave enough to take steps to improve their lives and for willingly sharing the stories that appear in the pages of this book.

Those weekends and this book could not have happened without the support of my friends who volunteered their time as facilitators. Thank you, angels – Steven, Caroline, Kevin, Patrick, Andrew, Pauline, Adrian, Sue, Mary, David, Clare, James, Lesley, Julia, Kerry, Nadja, Gary, Susan, Hannie, Marion, Arnoud, Denis, Kelly, Lynne, Kino-Kid, Philip, Leona, Pammie, Karen, Jag, Sarah and Paul.

And to PNB, thanks for the explorations, inspirations and the wild ride – long live luv 'n' lust!

A big thank you too to Paul McKenna, Michael Breen and Shelly Loughney. These last four years have been more fun than I could ever have imagined. Thank you for letting me hang out and continue to learn and develop.

I'd also like to congratulate my agent and friend, Philip Hodson, for believing in me, encouraging me and for negotiating a great deal!

A great big thanks to Lizzie Hutchings for helping shape this book into its best.

And finally, thank you to everyone who has entered my life at one time or another. All of you have had some effect on how I am today at my best, absolutely, living each moment with a joy for what is to come.

THE BEGINNING

WHAT DO WE MEAN BY 'FLIRTING' ANYWAY?

To start at the very beginning, let's define the word 'flirting' – or redefine it. If we didn't redefine things as we went along we'd all still be hunting for our meat and living in caves. Flirting comes from the old French word *fleurter*, meaning 'to flower'. Here are a few modern definitions from participants in my flirting classes:

- Flirting is about giving out that litte bit but not being totally available.
- Flirting is about fun, connecting and getting to know people.
- Flirting is a way of showing people you are interested in them.
- Flirting is about giving compliments, smiling and making people happy.
- Flirting is being like a butterfly – it flutters past in all its beauty and when we try to catch it, it flies away, leaving us wanting more. . .
- Flirting is eye contact. It's looking at people and smiling with your eyes.
- Flirting is making yourself so attractive that people can't resist you.
- Flirting is the art of being able to break down people's barriers and make contact.
- Flirting is being able to keep a conversation going after 'Hello'!

- Flirting is a great way to put a little sunshine in the world – or a lot!
- Flirting is showing people you are interested in them and making them feel warm towards you.
- Flirting is a harmless entertaining diversion that you can choose to take further if you wish.

Here's a mnemonic that sums up flirting for me:

F   Feeling good about yourself.

L   Liking other people.

I   Interesting people are interest-ed.

R   Rapport and resonance.

T   Talking their language.

I   Initiating conversation.

N   'No' means 'Go on to the next.' *No, next, no, next! Bingo! Yes!*

G   Giving great voice and loosening up your body.

Flirting is feeling great about yourself and resonating this to the world so that the right people are drawn to you irresistibly.

I call this 'SuccessFlirting' because you can use these skills to make a success of your social relationships and career as well as your love life!

THE BEST FLIRTS DO IT WITH EVERYONE!

This book is about how to be the kind of person who can flirt with anyone they choose! My friend Lesley is like that. She ran a business for 25 years, flirting with everyone. To this day she flirts with elderly people, children, babies, men and women. She flirts saucily with men she fancies and kindly with men she doesn't. She enjoys a joke and she can be really raunchy *and* very gentle. At the age of 48 she still has men chasing after her and she's been happily married for 26 years. Women consult her about their relationships and parents allow her to 'adopt' their children. There'll be standing room only at her funeral!

WHAT'S THE SECRET OF SUCCESSFUL FLIRTING?

So what's the secret of people like Lesley? In my research into truly successful flirts – SuccessFlirts! – I discovered that most of them have these traits in common:

- They know who they are.
- They have empowering beliefs about themselves and others.
- They see meeting people as opportunities to interact and feel good.
- They are able have a rapport with almost anyone and are flexible enough to bend and sway with the wind while maintaining their sense of themselves.
- They know that not everyone will love them, but they continue to view all people as interesting.
- They are upbeat and positive.
- They use language in ways that make others feel connected, willing and eager to participate.
- They have no aim in mind other than to make sure that when they have gained something, the other person has gained something too.
- They instinctively know that making other people feel good gives them great feelings too.
- They are in touch with and aware of their own reactions.
- They are in touch with and aware of their sexual energy.
- They pick up other people's signals and know when to take flirting to the next level and when to stop.
- They have fun and play like children.

I don't suppose you'd want to be like this, would you?!

BECOMING A FLIRT. . .

In this book you will learn how to develop all the qualities listed above. This is not a catalogue of flirting techniques or a dating guide; it doesn't tell you what to wear or say. It *is* about how to develop the confidence, attitudes, beliefs and skills to interact easily and successfully with yourself and others. Great flirts love who they are and what they do. This book is a guide and a collection of stories and explorations that will help you discover how wonderful you are *and* make you even better. It is about meeting yourself, growing to like and fall in love with yourself and learning to interact with the world from that basis.

This book is about how to flirt first with yourself and then with life, in such a way that people are drawn to you – irresistibly!

PART I: INSIDE

Good communication with others only comes once you have good communication with yourself, so first you will begin to work on yourself on the inside. In this section you will:

- uncover and enjoy what's great about yourself
- recognize the signals you give to yourself and others
- become aware of how you block yourself
- learn to adopt beliefs that empower you
- develop fantastic flirting states
- become more aware of your own body and voice as exquisite instruments of communication
- develop a sensory awareness of the silent messages you and others are sending out
- enjoy your sexuality and embrace it

PART II: OUTSIDE

Here you will learn skills that will help you interact successfully with people in the outside world. You will discover how to:

- radiate what is wonderful about you
- attract the right people to you
- develop a deep energetic rapport with people around you
- use language to influence and entice others

PART III: INTEGRATION

This section weaves together all that you have learned and takes you onwards as you begin to:

- create the future that is right for you
- discover the immense power of connecting and networking and how to integrate it into your life
- build up your flirting muscles by working through the 30-day programme at the end of the book

RESOURCES

This section lists books, tapes, courses, internet resources and people that can enhance your life.

Remember though, books don't jump out and change you overnight while you sleep. They offer you ways of thinking and acting that can help you to change yourself for the better. But you have to choose to do the work to make it happen!

Do you want to choose to be a SuccessFlirt? Let's start now!

INSIDE *part one*

CHAPTER 1

SUCCESSFLIRTING —*a way of life*

WHERE DOES FLIRTING BEGIN?

The secret of great flirting is to begin on the inside, with yourself! The better you know yourself, the easier it is for you to flirt successfully and love it. Do you know how wonderful you are?

Great flirts know who they are, rejoice in it and are honest about it. They feel good about themselves and transmit that to others. If you want to be like this, it's important that you begin to know more about who you are and to be proud of it.

WHO ARE YOU?

YOUR STORY

So, who do you think you are? This is how some of the participants on one of my flirting workshops answered this question:

'I am a computer programmer.'
'I am 27.'

'I am a black woman.'

'I am gay.'

'I am a mother and wife.'

'I am a divorcée.'

'I am a reluctant accountant.'

'I'm shy.'

'I'm a nerd.'

'I'm a bit boring really.'

'I'm an old hippie.'

'I'm Mrs Smith.'

Some people define themselves by their work, some by their sexuality or their role in life or their relationship to others. Nearly everyone defines themselves in relation to some slot in the world. That's pretty limited in my opinion. I don't think anyone can define themselves by one thing.

OTHER PEOPLE'S STORIES

Sometimes – even worse – we take on the definitions other people have created for us. As we grow up, we absorb the messages from those around us about how life should be and how *we* should be. As a result others can unconsciously drain our enthusiasm for what naturally attracts us. Some of us give up dreaming our own dreams and concentrate on trying to fit a mould created for us by someone else. Slowly we learn how *not* to be the way we were meant to be.

We all come in with character and calling. But the fog of birth obscures this self-understanding.

James Hillman, *The Soul's Code*

Many of us end up living in fear of what others might say if we don't live up to what we believe is 'expected', 'traditional' or 'right'. Some people come on my flirting courses and don't want their friends to know what they are doing. But there should be no shame in wanting more out of your life. Shame comes from being programmed to believe that what other people think about you is more important than being yourself. The real shame is in ignoring what is inside you waiting to come out and living a life that is not the one for you.

But if you have not lived up to the ideals set for yourself by other people, you have not failed. You have realized that there is more out there! Great! Congratulate yourself!

The moment you begin to create your own definition of a successful life is the moment you begin to succeed.

I love this story about Oprah Winfrey. One day Oprah's grandmother decided to teach her how to wash clothes because she believed Oprah would be doing someone's washing some day. Oprah recounts how she heard a voice inside her head saying, 'You will never have to do this. You will become somebody.' And she did. She is now one of the most powerful women in the world, using her power more and more to help others set themselves free. She knows who she is – and it's not a label someone else created for her.

I don't think of myself as a poor, deprived ghetto girl who made good. I think of myself as somebody who from an early age knew I was responsible for myself and I had to make good.
Oprah Winfrey

YOUR TRUE STORY

So, who are you? What kind of person are you? Would you like to explore who you are?

There are 'explorations' throughout this book. As you participate in them, you will be encouraged to question yourself and experiment with your brain and your body. You may find yourself out of your comfort zone. Good. In the East they believe that discomfort means you are about to learn. They welcome it! If you feel uncomfortable at any time, ask yourself: 'What is going on here? What's the message? What do I need to find out? What am I learning?' That way you will realize the value of the experience. Sometimes you may agree or disagree with what I am saying. When this happens, ask yourself whether it is a true difference of opinion or a knee-jerk reaction, and if so, what can you learn from it?

Remember, though, that it's not all hard work! As well as what you learn consciously, as you read through this book you will be unconsciously absorbing information, because wrapped in its folds are many ideas that will just go in and pop up as new awareness or behaviour days, weeks or even months later.

As you read and do the explorations, check with yourself:

- ♥ Have you found out more about yourself?
- ♥ Do you feel more hopeful?
- ♥ Are you a tiny bit closer to what you want for yourself?
- ♥ Have you learned something useful?
- ♥ Are you keen to find out even more?

You might like to keep a special notebook for your explorations. Writing something down often clarifies what's in your head and sometimes the act itself is enough to trigger a small change. It is also useful to keep notes so that you can look back on them later and see how far you have come. Twelve years ago, I described my ideal day and now I find a lot of this has come true. It's magical to look back and realize that it is possible not just to change but to create the life you want.

Find somewhere quiet to do your first exploration. If you are somewhere busy now, make a note to find some time to do this exploration before you read on.

WHO ARE YOU?

What kind of person are you?
Write down what comes into your head when you read the question. Sense it and let it flow. Remember, when you are honest with yourself, there is no right or wrong, there is just what is. . .

To give you some idea, when I did exploration myself I wrote quite a lot and here's some of it:

I am a person who loves animals. I write, I run groups and get a buzz from spending time with my cat, hanging out on the Internet and being with friends. I love coaching people to realize more of who they are. I am highly flirtatious and a voracious networker. I enjoy the time I spend with my lover and I love my own company. I like adventures and relish good food. I enjoy walking along an empty beach with the sun on my back getting a sense of being at one with the world. I'm creative and wild and I am passionate about changing the world.

Now read what you wrote and as you read, notice what feelings you get in your body. Notice where they are. It's important to be aware of your feelings and we'll be doing a lot of this along the way, so we might as well start now!

When you have finished reading this book, ask yourself this question again. You may find that you have discovered even more about the real you hiding beneath the layers we have peeled away . . .

Now you have defined who you are, you have to know what you want, otherwise how will you know if you've got it? Here's another exploration.

WHAT DO YOU REALLY, REALLY WANT?

Is there something you have been longing to do? What are those big dreams, those deep wishes and desires that you harbour deep inside? If you were to wake up tomorrow and find a miracle had happened, what would your life be like?

What do you want? Describe how it will be for you.

- ♥ Reread what you have written.
- ♥ If there is a lot of detail, take each individual item you have listed and ask: 'What will this get me?'

Why should you let go of what you want? It may seem strange, but once you know what you want and then let go of it, opportunities will open out for you. I don't know why, but people who continually worry about getting what they want seem to struggle harder than those who let go and just get on with having a good time.

Many of the participants on my courses and private clients have one thing in common. They are desperate. They say things like 'I must find a backer for my project' or 'I need a relationship.' They are focusing very strongly on what they want. But narrowing your focus so much means that you miss out on other things that may indirectly lead you to what you want.

CLOSED DOWN OR OPENED OUT?

Imagine this scenario. Liz goes to a party intent on finding a man. She looks around at the party and, not seeing a 'decent' man, loses interest. She goes home early. Now imagine this scenario. Liz goes to a party intent on having a good time and connecting with interesting people. She gets chatting to a woman who invites her to a wine tasting. At the wine tasting she meets someone who is also passionate about theatre and happens to live near Liz. Liz goes to the theatre with her new friend and is introduced to Alan, who is an acquaintance of the new friend's husband. Alan and Liz get chatting. . . Need I go on? When Liz chooses to 'let go' of her desire to find a man, she is free to make other connections that can lead she knows not where. If we don't connect, we don't open the doors to opportunity. So, let go of your dreams, be aware of them and place them somewhere safe. Life is an adventure. Instead of trying to stick to a plan, let it unfold as it is meant to.

Also, when you concentrate on larger-scale ideas, like being in a harmonious relationship rather than specifying the desired partner's hair colour, height and professional status, you are opening yourself to more opportunities to flirt and connect.

At this stage it may seem as though your dreams will never become reality, but many people have already reprogrammed themselves for flirting success. Marie, for instance, had held back from going after what she wanted, but when she discovered her best self, she gained a place at business school, joined a dating agency and found a man! Paul wanted to be more sexually attractive. With his newfound confidence he attracted Rita, a sociable, sexy woman who was just right for him. Geoff saw brick walls between himself and women he liked. He learned to remove his imaginary barriers and feel confident enough to ask a girl for a date. You can make your dreams come true as well!

JEFF'S STORY:
Flirting his Way to Success

For some people SuccessFlirting truly is a way of life. Jeff Cain, for example, is one of the most accomplished flirts I've ever known. His zest for life is exhilarating and energizes everyone around him. Back in 1980 Jeff was one of an élite few who had an answering machine and he turned his message into a chat show! At a time when you were lucky if you could get one in ten callers to leave a message, Jeff's number got passed round the UK and soon the phone line was jammed with people wanting to leave messages. At the prompting of a friend, I rang up and found myself listening to him for 20 minutes, laughing most of the time. Eventually Jeff and I became great friends.

Jeff put out something that excited and amused others and pulled them into his orbit. And he loved meeting new people. He invited himself to parties, he kept in touch with people, he did things for them. He connected constantly.

When you connect with people, you never know where it will lead.

When Jeff wasn't being interested in other people, he was sharing his dreams and ideas with anyone who would listen. Eventually he set up one of the UK's first telephone chat and entertainment services. It was a resounding success. Jeff just did what he loved and started a business around it. He was a success in all areas of his life, but he worked hard at it. He put in the energy and reaped the rewards. Beneath all this, he truly liked who he was and believed in himself.

This was what drew people to him. He was the kind of person people loved to have around. He brought sunshine into everyone's lives – including mine!

Jeff was also one of the most charismatic women-magnets I've ever met! After all, who wouldn't want to be with someone so charged up with a zest for life? When you learn to give out that charge, you'll find yourself pulling people towards you, too!

WHAT ABOUT YOU?

SuccessFlirting is a way of life for Jeff and countless others like him, and it can be for you. It is simply about feeling great about who you are and spreading it to other people, which makes them feel great too. When people feel great they are open to suggestions, opportunities and invitations. Their hearts, minds and support become available to you because you give genuine value to them.

Soon you will be making connections with people in ways you never dreamed possible. It's your choice, your journey. I'm here to guide you and motivate you to do it for yourself.

Do you want to feel better on a daily basis and begin to make others feel good too? What's your answer – 'yes' or 'yes'?

Wherever you are in your life right now, remember that the best thing about the past is that it has passed away . . . and the best thing about the future is that it is waiting for you to arrive – and to love every minute of it.

EXPLORE YOUR FLIRTING PATTERNS

As a SuccessFlirt you will be able to make things happen *for* you, not *to* you. You will make things happen *because* of what you do, not *despite* what you do. What do you do now? You may have some patterns of behaviour that don't serve you and some that do. Let's explore your current flirting patterns.

HOW DO YOU FLIRT?

Perhaps you are a bit of a flirt already. Perhaps you flirt but don't get the results you want. Perhaps you don't flirt at all. This exploration is designed solely to enhance your self-awareness, which is why there is no interpretation at the end. You are capable of realizing what you need to work on, aren't you?!

You are in a relaxed social situation and realize you are attracted to someone. Do you:

- Send out strong sexual signals and if they don't approach you, approach them?
- Flirt with someone else while occasionally looking in their direction?
- Hope that they don't notice you are interested and be certain to look away?

A guy came over to talk to me once as I stood outside a seminar room. He asked me about the seminar. I felt a strong physical attraction to him. After chatting for a while, I gave him my card and walked downstairs, as the seminar was about to begin. Halfway down, I turned round, walked back up the stairs and asked him if we could go for a ride on his motorbike. We are still seeing each other! Sometimes you have to follow your instincts and not worry about the consequences. I didn't stop to think this guy might refuse me or think I was too pushy – I just went for it!

You are in a fairly well populated train carriage. A personable, well presented person gets into the carriage and strikes up a conversation. Do you:

- Say 'Good evening' and return to your paper or your work?
- Ignore them – after all, they might be a bore or a rapist?
- Open out to the possibilities and strike up a conversation?

Fran was directing a TV documentary about my seminar. She told me that after spending an afternoon with me, she was feeling really chirpy. On the train home, a man got into her carriage, smiled and said, 'Hello.' Normally, Fran would have mumbled an indistinct greeting, looked away and got on with her work. This time, she remembered something I'd said about feeling good and connecting, and she smiled back and made a comment about a topical event. During the course of the subsequent conversation the pair discovered they were both in the TV business, lived in the same town *and* he knew her husband. They exchanged telephone numbers and made plans to meet up for dinner with their partners. Who knows where this friendship will lead?

We can't expect to meet new friends, lovers and business contacts through the usual channels. Sometimes it's our willingness to take advantage of unlikely situations that leads us to wonderful friendships, a new relationship or that great business opportunity.

You know that it is your boss's birthday and you like him or her. Do you:

- Send an appropriate card and/or make a point of wishing them a great day and genuinely be interested in if and how they are celebrating?
- Ignore it – you're not a brown-noser?
- Sign a general card if it comes round, but keep any comments very formal?

I shared my birthday with a female boss. My partner at the time sent me an orchid at work *and* he sent her one too. She wasn't the kind of person open to 'bribery' and flattery, but it sure put a glow on her face that day and she passed it on to us. My partner hadn't ever stopped to think that perhaps he shouldn't make the gesture. He genuinely liked my boss and wanted to make her feel good. When we follow our instincts to be nice instead of some silly so-called 'rules' we create about what is right and what is not, we give out a glow to others that can only have a positive effect.

You know that someone you have met recently but don't know too well could connect you to someone who would be very useful to you in your business. Do you:

- Ring up that person, ask them how they are, listen to what they say, make them feel good and then say honestly that you know they can help you and that's why you are calling?
- Ring them up about another matter and hope that one thing will lead to another?
- Stop yourself from calling because it would seem like using them?

Sue attended one of my personal development events in London. She called me up the next day, thanked me for the evening and then told me that she knew that I was an influential person and had a far wider reach in the personal development community than she did. She told me a story that really made me laugh and asked if I would publicize her coaching. I asked her to give me a session, she agreed and I did publicize her because she was good.

Sue was pro-active, funny and friendly. She had made me feel good without flattery and she was genuine and prepared to put herself on the line because she believed in herself.

As a result of reading this, I suspect that you may have become more aware of how flirtatious you are. Would you like to be more pro-active, talk more often to strangers and be able to socialize in any situation? Have there been times in your life when you could have made a great connection, but didn't? If so, this book is for you.

A UNIVERSAL CHALLENGE

As a communication therapist I have worked with many people with a variety of challenges. Everyone wants to make some changes. Some of them are really stuck. They say things like 'I can't flirt', 'I don't know what to say', 'I flirt too much', 'I'm not good enough', 'I'm too ugly.' Some of their stories follow. As you read stories, you might recognize something of yourself in them.

Although most of the following examples are about relationship flirting, the characteristics are common to people who have challenges in general social communication in all areas of life.

GERI'S STORY: *'Why Should I Flirt When I'm Good at What I Do?'*

Geri was a successful advertising executive who felt she had had to fight her way to her current position. She was good at what she did and in her own words she didn't 'tolerate fools'. She had been passed over for an account directorship which had gone to Adele, a woman whom Geri considered frivolous. When pressed, Geri admitted that Adele was a brilliant account executive, but she thought she didn't take things seriously enough and spent too much time 'fooling around'. Geri equated success in her career with being tough and serious. She thought that she had to suppress her feminine qualities in order to succeed.

What's the Message Here?

Geri realized that if she had allowed herself to have more fun, she might have been more popular. When she asked a colleague what Adele had that she didn't, she was told: 'Adele is like a ray of sunshine. She's so easy to work with because she makes everything seem like fun.' Geri learnt the hard way that having fun and success in business are compatible.

Might you be taking life too seriously and denying yourself some fun – and success?

RACHEL'S STORY: *'If They Think I'm Sexy, They'll Like Me'*

Rachel confessed to me that her great flirting secret was to 'think about dirty sex, stare at someone and if they don't react, pull them towards me'. 'The only trouble,' she whined, 'is that they all want sex and all I want most of the time is a drink.'

14   **FLIRT COACH**

Rachel was a classic sexual flirt. She thought the only way she could attract the attention of a man was to promise sex. So she turned it on full blast and then wondered why men always made a grab for her.

What's the Message Here?

Sexuality is a primary driving force in all humans. We can use it beautifully and exquisitely when the time is right to draw someone to us. There are also times when it isn't appropriate or fair to flirt sexually.

Be honest, are there times when you've used your sexuality to get what you want and what you want isn't sex? What might be the dangers of this? Is it worth it?

NAOMI: *Daren't Flirt*

Naomi, on the other hand, was terrified of flirting for fear of the reaction it would cause. She went out once with a man she quite liked and when they kissed, he got an erection. Naomi ran a mile! She was scared of the power of her sexuality and she saw the man's reaction as a sign that he was bound to expect sex.

What's the Message Here?

Somewhere along the line someone had told Naomi that men were uncontrollable animals and women must temper their behaviour so as not to arouse their animal instincts.

When Naomi learnt to feel good about herself, she also learnt to accept that it is natural for men to be sexually attracted to women. Instead of seeing herself as a wicked temptress, she was grateful that she was a sexy desirable woman.

Do you repress your sexuality for fear of what it might arouse? How is this serving you?

LEANNE:
Safety First Flirt

Leanne was quite good at flirting – with the wrong men. If she liked someone she wouldn't flirt with them for fear of being rejected. Instead she flirted with people who seemed interested in her. She flirted herself into a string of 'wrong' relationships ending in an unhappy marriage and a nasty divorce.

What's the Lesson Here?
Leanne learned that she needed to go for what she wanted instead of what she thought was her lot.

Are you scared to show someone you like them? Do you flirt with 'safe' men?

CHRIS:
The Androgynous Flirt

Chris was Mr Nice. He always ended up as a friend but never the boyfriend. He had no problem asking women out, but he never got as far as taking the relationship to a more sexual level. He spent so much time being Mr Nice he forgot how to be Mr Sexy. Women like a mixture of both!

What's the Lesson Here?
Chris learned that he could turn up his sexual meter a little and send different messages to women.

Are you being too much of a nice guy and forgetting you are a sexual being too?

LISA:
'They Won't Want to Talk to Little Me'

Lisa came into daily contact with powerful and famous people as part of her work. When she was at work and was one to one with people she felt great and 'in control', but when she had to go to socialite parties, she suddenly dried up. Everyone in the room seemed more important, more interesting and more fun than her.

FLIRT COACH

Lisa felt good when she had the backup of her work to give her status. Once she was no longer in control, she lost her confidence. She built up pictures of people rejecting her overtures or finding her conversation boring. Lisa's mother had always pointed out lively people at parties and called them 'show offs'. . .

What's the Lesson Here?

Lisa learned to love herself more and to expect others to value her company and opinions. She learned to 'flirt with life'.

How highly do you value yourself? Are you too modest and self-effacing?

Everyone has their challenges and the people in these stories learned to make changes and come out feeling great. You can too!

But first let's look at some evidence that explains why this way of working is successful. I invite you to come with me to explore the science of emotion. . .

CHAPTER 2

THE SCIENCE OF *emotion*

EMOTIONS AND FLIRTING

To flirt effectively, you have to feel good about yourself and be in a positive state of mind. This means you need to have more positive emotions more often. In order to achieve this, you have to know how you do it naturally so that you can repeat it – even on bad days!

STORING EMOTIONS

Dr Candace Pert has proved that our body stores the physical memories of both bad and good emotions in our cells by changing their format.

Pert showed that bodies have pockets of 'information receptors' located everywhere. The strongest clusters of these receptors are located around the entry point for the five senses, i.e. nose, mouth, eyes, ears and skin. Each receptor is programmed to receive and bind with specific transmitters of information – the chemicals running through our bodies as we experience different emotions. As the receptors and transmitters bind, they set off a chain reaction and the cells start to change. If we are angry, the modifications to the cells are completely different from those that occur when we are happy.

So, the more we experience good emotions, the better memories our bodies have. We literally embody our emotions for good or ill! Which would you prefer to do?

YOUR BODY CAN RECALL EVERY STORED MEMORY!

According to Pert's theory, your body stores in chemical codes the memory of every great sexual experience, every amazing sunset, every wondrous event that has literally raised the hairs of your arms and sent tingling sensations through your entire body. Every one is stored in memory and can be reactivated. . .

JEMIMA'S STORY:
An Experience Relived

Jemima meditates quite a lot. When I asked her what it was like to meditate she said, 'I feel so composed.' As she spoke, her hands moved up and she went into what appeared to be a very quiet, composed, calm state. Her breathing slowed down, her voice softened and she stood in a very balanced way.

Jemima wasn't just *talking about* being composed. She was *doing* composed. Her body was creating a complete state of 'composed' based on Information she was 're-membering' – putting back in the limbs   by moving her body into a 'composed' position.

We don't just remember experiences in our head, we do them in our body.

What would it be like if you could re-member a particular state of mind again and again? How might that affect your ability to feel good more often? And how might that affect your ability to flirt naturally?

STRUCTURING MEMORIES

The way we choose to structure our memories has an effect on the emotions that we create around them. When you are aware of this, you can learn to change the feelings a memory gives you by changing *how* you remember it.

We'll do more of that later. It's great for changing how we feel about rejection and past hurts and for 'amping' up the good feelings and having more of them. And of course when you can do that you create the right state of mind for flirting and having more fun! For now, this exploration will enable you to experience a memory in different ways.

PLAYING WITH YOUR EXPERIENCE

Before you start, here's how you structure experiences. When you think of an experience, you always make some kind of image in your mind's eye (that's what that phrase means!) It might not be very clear, but you have a definite sense of it and should be able to describe what you 'see'. If you doubt this, ask yourself what colour your front door is. To answer that you must refer to some mental image so that you could see the colour, even if just for a second!

Also, when you think of an experience, you get physical sensations. These are the result of the chemical and cellular changes occurring in your body due to the stimulus of the experience. They can be tingly feelings, heavy feelings, stabbing feelings, buzzy feelings or other sorts of feelings and you get them in specific areas of your body. Be aware of the feelings you get as you do this exploration.

- ♥ Think of a time when you were having a really juicy experience.
- ♥ Imagine you are actually reliving the experience, as if seeing it through your own eyes. It is going on around you. You are in it. *How does that affect the feelings you are getting in your body?*
- ♥ Now, count to 10 and imagine the same experience, but this time imagine you are watching a movie of it. You are no longer in it, but observing yourself in it. *How are the feelings different this time?*

You will probably notice that when you enter fully into an experience the physical feelings in your body are stronger and when you stand back from it they become weaker.

When we recall events as if we are in them, experiencing them, we are *associated* with the experience. When we watch ourselves experiencing an event from afar, we are *dissociated* from it.

You can use association and dissociation to make your memories weaker or more powerful.

BAD MEMORIES VS. GOOD MEMORIES

You may have memories of particular situations where someone rejected you or criticized you. If these memories are strong and vivid, when you recall them you are probably associating fully with them as if they are actually happening all over again and they may be causing you unnecessary pain, literally, in the form of uncomfortable feelings somewhere in your body.

The great news is that you can learn to dissociate from the bad memories and the feelings will get weaker. You can also associate more fully with the good ones. This makes the good ones more powerful.

The more you remember the good times and let the bad times fade into the distance, the better you will feel about yourself – and the more naturally flirtatious you will become!

TAKING RESPONSIBILITY FOR OUR FEELINGS

We must take responsibility for what we feel. The notion that others can make us feel good or bad is untrue.

Candace Pert, *Molecules of Emotion*

To recap, our physical feelings are our experience of the chemical and physiological changes occurring in our body as a result of our emotions. A feeling of sinking in the stomach, for example, is due to a concentration of a chemical in that area created by our reaction to a situation. As that happens, our cells are storing the information. Most of this happens unconsciously, but when we become aware of it, we can begin to change it consciously, just as we can change our breathing.

Our body knows how to breathe, of course. Most of the time we let our autonomic system get on with it. But sometimes it's useful to regulate our breathing. Yoga exercises encourage measured, rhythmic slow breathing. Pregnant women control their breathing in order to counteract pain and when people get panicky they are encouraged to pause for a moment and take a deep breath.

In the same way that we can take conscious control of our breath to change the way we feel, so we can take conscious control of how we structure our emotions and change them.

We can become responsible for creating our own feelings.

FEELING GOOD

Good flirts don't depend on other people to feel good, they create their own good times and spread them around!

GERRY'S STORY:
'I Needed Her to Feel Good'

Gerry wrote to me asking how he could make a first date work so that he got a relationship. By the end of his letter he said:

I was hoping that if I went out with her I would start to feel good but then I realized I should feel good enough anyway and would like some help with this.

Gerry realized that he should be able to create his own good feelings and not have to rely on someone else to create them for him. He was beginning to tackle his problems himself instead of relying on someone else to make him feel good – which is always a rather hit and miss affair.

SUSAN'S STORY:
'He Made Me Feel Bad'

Susan came to see me because she wanted to stop being obsessed with her ex-husband. She would imagine him with his new girlfriend, living in their house and laughing about her, and she would feel really bad.

At first she believed she was not responsible for her feelings, *he* was. But when she realized how much power she had given him on a plate, she decided to take it back.

Susan was running through a certain pattern of feelings in her body whenever she thought of her ex-husband and when she learned to change that and re-member the experience in a different way, she felt better. That paved the way for her to be more flirtatious – and she got healthier!

And that reminds me – flirting is healthy.

FLIRTING GETS YOU HIGH

It's official! In 1999 scientific studies were made of people who flirted. It was discovered that after a flirting encounter, their blood had considerably increased levels of endorphins, opiates, immuno-globulin, white blood cells and lots of other natural immune-boosting chemicals. These people got high on flirting – legally!

Wouldn't it be great if you could learn to create that flirting high at will? Good news! You can.

YOU CAN INCREASE YOUR WHITE BLOOD CELL COUNT

Here's some more proof that the mind has an effect on the body. In one experiment which explored the immune system and our control over it, scientists discovered that we literally boost our immune system by the way we think. Children were asked to imagine their white blood cells as policemen going round their body chasing the baddies away. As they really got into the game and began to imagine more and more policemen, the number of white blood cells in their blood actually went up. They had amped up the power of their immune system with the power of thought alone!

YOU CAN INCREASE BLOOD FLOW

In scientific tests in which people were asked to visualize blood flowing to body parts, they recorded significantly increased blood flow in those parts. How useful could that be when you get past flirting to the next stage?!

LOVING FEELINGS BOOST YOUR IMMUNITY

What happens when you think loving or even lusty thoughts? Two Harvard psychologists, David McClelland and Carol Kirshnit, conducted an experiment in 1982. They tested the saliva of people who watched movies about love and discovered that the level of an antibody known as immunoglobulin-A increased significantly for up to an hour after each film had finished. The effect was extended if the subjects recalled times when they had received tender loving care from someone.

You can boost your immune system just by *remembering* good experiences (and you can boost them even more by *doing* them!)

Here is evidence that loving thoughts and moods actually increase antibody production. But more to the point, imagine what we are doing if we are emotionally negative . . . That doesn't bear thinking about, does it?

LAUGHTER, THE BEST MEDICINE

Great flirts spend more time laughing and smiling than other people. I'm sure you'll agree that a laughing person is more attractive than a frowning one. So, you can boost your immune system at the same time as you boost your desirability! Laughter is indeed the best medicine.

LAUGHTER: VITAMIN L

When you laugh, a chemical is released in your body which literally sets off a chain reaction of cellular change. Each time you laugh you are creating a positive cell memory in your body as you release opiates and endorphins, the body's good-time drugs.

SMILING: VITAMIN S

Great flirts will tell you that the more you smile, the more you are saying to the outside world, 'I am not a black cloud to be avoided, I am a sunshine person. Come bask in my rays . . .'

FAKE IT TILL YOU MAKE IT

You can start with a fake smile and it will eventually turn into a real one.

💜 Try it now. Just turn up the corners of your mouth and put on a smile. . .
Keep it going, make it wider. It doesn't matter if anyone is looking. *Smile now!*

💜 And pay attention to your body from head to toe. How are you sitting –
are you comfortable? Is there anywhere in your body that is tense? Just
noticing these things can help you to relax. Sometimes when I am sitting
around, I find my left hand is screwed up into a semi-fist and just by
checking it from time to time, I can relax it and release the tension.

💜 Make a note of your feelings.

YOUR FEELING PATTERN

Learning to evoke good feelings at will is crucial to becoming a consummate
flirt. We can do this when we become more aware of how our body works. The
next few explorations will help you get more in touch with how your body
translates emotions into good and bad feelings.

YOUR BASE STATE

Before you begin, just check around your body. This is a base state. Check
out how it is for you:

💜 What's going on in your stomach?
💜 Are your shoulders hunched or relaxed?
💜 Does your chest feel tight or expanded?
💜 Are your hands clenched or loose?
💜 Are you frowning or is your face relaxed?
💜 Are your legs or ankles crossed or uncrossed?

Notice any difference when you change from one stance to another.

Now you know that your body holds feelings in certain places you can relax.

You will have your own feeling pattern for different feelings. There are unlimited variations. A feeling will start somewhere in your body and probably move somewhere else. Feelings are constantly in motion – 'e-motions'.

For example, when Susan thought about her ex-husband she got a kind of banging in her forehead which was followed by her throat clenching and swallowing, a tight sick feeling in her stomach and her heart beating faster. She also found that her shoulders were hunched up to her neck. These were her 'bad-time feelings'.

You are going to find out what yours are.

BAD-TIME FEELINGS

First, think of a time when you experienced bad feelings or emotions which were not useful to you. Avoid really traumatic issues here! Maybe choose a time when you wanted to approach someone but didn't and felt bad about it or a time when you were late and got stressed out or when you got a brush-off.

Take a moment to just relive the experience and as you do so, notice the feelings you are getting.

- ♥ Where are the feelings located? Chest, stomach, front of the head, back of the neck?
- ♥ What type of sensations are they? Prickly? Buzzing? Tight? Heavy? or . . . Which 'feeling' word would you choose to describe the sensation?
- ♥ Where are they going? Which direction are they going in?
- ♥ Do they have a rhythm? Are they, for example, fast or slow, gentle or strong, pulsating or stabbing? Which word would you choose to describe the sensation?

Now come back to your base state and think about what you did or didn't have for breakfast . . . and now *smile* . . . because you are going to get the opportunity to compare the bad-time feelings with good-time ones.

GOOD-TIME FEELINGS

Think of one of the most stupendous experiences of your life. It could be any sort of experience – some time spent in nature or an interaction with someone special or a feeling of accomplishment. Whatever it is, pick a time when you felt absolutely amazing!

Now notice where the feelings are for that kind of experience.

💜 Where are the feelings located? Chest, stomach, front of the head, back of the neck?

💜 What type of sensations are they? Prickly? Buzzing? Tight? Heavy? or . . . Which 'feeling' word would you choose to describe the sensation?

💜 Where are they going? Which direction are they going in?

💜 Do they have a rhythm? Are they fast or slow, gentle or strong, pulsating or stabbing? Which word would you choose to describe the sensation?

💜 Can you describe the sensation in general? Perhaps you have a word for it?

I trust you noticed some difference between your good-time and bad-time feelings. This is a first step towards being aware of what goes on in your body.

You now know that your body can recall physically both bad and good memories and you can access them at will. The next chapter is about how to use your senses fully to become instinctively more aware of what is going on for you and for others.

CHAPTER 3

SHARPENING UP *your senses*

THE VALUE OF SHARP SENSES

Sensory acuity is the backbone of good communication.

In order to flirt with others, you need to be able to communicate with them. And good communication with others depends on how well you communicate with yourself. Without it, all the flirting techniques in the world will not help you.

You have already had some experience of becoming more aware of your feelings. In order to communicate better with yourself, you also need to sharpen up your senses. Your senses are the media through which you pick up both your own and other people's signals. The more you can sense, the easier you will find it to flirt right on in there.

Great flirts are experts at unconsciously picking up small signals and 'tracking' the patterns of people they flirt with:

- Someone who is a good listener knows when a person has paused and takes up their cue to enter the conversation. They note the words people use and play them back to them.
- Someone who has acute vision notices little changes in facial movement, skin tone or bodily gestures.
- Someone who feels things often gets intuitive answers as to what move to make next.
- Someone with an acute sense of smell notices subtle changes in body odour.

When you are able to sense how another person is feeling, you will know when to move more quickly or slowly – or, indeed, when to stop and move on!

USING ALL THE SENSES

I often go running along the seafront where I live. Before starting my run, I decide which sense I want to concentrate on developing. One day I pay attention to the sounds around me, the next I concentrate on what I can see. This way I have really begun to notice new things. I have also realized which of my senses I need to sharpen up.

You can adapt this exploration to your everyday routine and do it as often as you like!

'SENSADAY' WORKOUT

Next time you go out alone for a walk or a run might be an ideal time to try this out. A natural setting, even a city park, is an interesting place to do this as it has so much to offer the senses in terms of pleasant input. You might want to use the same spot and sense it differently over a period of time. This way you can notice how much more you sense over the days and how this adds to the richness of your experience.

DAY 1: VISION

You can begin by paying special attention to the sights around you. Describe what you see. Are there trees? What colour are their leaves? Notice the intensity of the different colours. Look out for people, buildings, all the little details. . .

DAY 2: SOUND

Today you can decide to spend some time concentrating on the sounds around you. When I go on my run, I am aware of the wind whistling, of the leaves rustling and the sound of the ocean, the background noises of traffic and even the sound of my breathing. Keep your ears open and listen.

DAY 3: TOUCH AND FEELING

Concentrate on what you can feel. When the sun shines you may feel warmth. If it is hot you may sense the slight dampness of sweat emerging from your pores or perhaps you can feel the breeze or the texture of your clothes on your skin. This is easy to get to grips with once you start.

DAY 4: SMELL

Today you can concentrate on smells. When I run by the sea, I notice the smell of the sea, of the seaweed, of a cigarette as I pass by someone smoking and the different smells of the greenery, but if you are in the city, you might smell the petrol of cars, a newly mown lawn, the creosote on a fence, the honeysuckle from a garden. . . Often when we notice unpleasant smells around us we close down our sense of smell. Be open to all smells, even the 'unpleasant' ones.

DAY 5: TASTE

You can practise this exercise each time you eat a meal. Begin by saying to yourself that you are going to look for the taste of all the ingredients in whatever you are eating. Identify them. You might think that taste only works with edible objects, but later as you perk up your taste buds, you will begin to appreciate lots more tasty things.

When you continue to do this as a regular exercise and concentrate on different senses for a set amount of time each day, you will notice your senses becoming more acute and you will begin to notice more about the world around you *and* the people around you.

A WORD ABOUT SMELL

Smell is the only sense that connects directly to the brain's cortex and it is very evocative. I am sure there are smells that bring back memories for you. For me a certain suntan lotion reminds me of a particular trip abroad.

Each of us has a unique smell. Our body is a chemical factory which is constantly mixing different concoctions. We all send out chemicals called pheromones. When we are afraid we smell differently from when we are happy or ecstatic or sexually aroused.

We are attracted to people by their smell. Perhaps there's someone you care for whose smell makes you feel good. My friend Susan says that she loves the natural smell of her partner. Equally, we can be repelled. Have you ever been close to someone and just not liked their smell, and it wasn't because they had body odour, more something you couldn't identify but just knew?

Sometimes you will find yourself drawn to people by a mixture of sight, smell and feelings. We are all attracted by things that appeal to our different senses.

A WORD ABOUT INTERPRETATION

Please remember, however, that developing a greater awareness of the signals people give out will not turn you into a magic interpreter of their emotions. So, if you catch yourself saying things like 'He looked happy' or 'She was bored', *stop*. Be careful about making interpretations. Ever had someone tell you to cheer up when you weren't miserable? They mistakenly interpreted a set of signals as an emotion. Isn't it annoying? Most of the time it happens to me, it's because I am lost in thought, *not* miserable!

Being able to recognize changes in the sensory signals you and others emit will give you a starting-point. But before you go on to even consider interpreting the signals other people give out, you need to be aware of what your own senses are telling you about yourself. This is another step towards becoming a great flirt.

COMING TO YOUR SENSES

If you don't like your reality – change it.

Richard Bandler

We don't just see, hear, feel, touch, smell or taste the world – we do it in much more detail. If you think of your senses as the main building blocks of your internal experience, the detail is the structure of those building blocks.

When we conjure up events in our mind we use our senses to depict them in certain ways. We don't just hear a sound, we hear a type of sound. We don't just get one feeling, we have different types of feelings. If we make a picture in our mind's eye it can be panoramic, framed, small, large, bright, dim, near or far, black and white or colour, moving or still. If we talk to ourselves, the voice can have a direction, it can be near or far, loud or soft, high and shrill or low and sexy, slow or fast. If we feel something it can be in many different locations in our body, heavy or sharp, buzzy or dull.

SuccessFlirts make images that are positive and motivational, life-size and in full colour with great sounds, and they see them through their own eyes. They envisage the world working out positively for them. They talk to themselves encouragingly in nice voices and so give themselves great feelings. This sets them up for going out there and flirting with anyone.

Unfortunately, when it comes to thinking about interacting with other people, especially people we are attracted to, many of us seem to have an amazing ability to construct larger than life full-colour Hammer Horror movies instead! No wonder that this does *not* create great feelings.

It stands to reason that if we have the imagination to create a doomsday scenario for ourselves, we can use exactly the same mechanism to create a wonderful happy ending in our mind's eye. When we do that, we are setting ourselves up for success.

In order to create your own wonderful movies it is essential to understand the building blocks of your own experiences. That's the subject of the next exploration.

HOW DO YOU STRUCTURE YOUR EXPERIENCES?

Think of a situation which was really enjoyable.

While you experience the memory of this enjoyable situation, you can get detailed information on how you structure your experiences by answering the questions below. It doesn't matter if you can't answer all of these, but you will get answers to some. (And don't worry if you think you can't visualize. You can. You know what colour your front door is, don't you?) Now think of that juicy experience again.

VISION

- Are there several images or just one?
- Is it like a movie or a still photograph?
- Is it in colour or black and white?
- Is it brighter or darker than real life?
- Is it in focus or is it blurred or fuzzy?
- Is there a border round the edge or is it a wide-angle panoramic picture?
- Are you watching yourself in the scene or are you seeing it through your own eyes?
- Is it bigger or smaller than real life or is it life-size?
- Is it flat or three-dimensional?
- Does the picture wrap around you?
- Is it close or far away?
- Where is it? Which direction are you seeing it from (in front, to the side, above you, below)?

You are beginning to work out the structure of your experience and soon you'll be able to change it. Sounds cool? It is!

Now that you have worked out the visual submodalities of this very enjoyable experience, you can have a go at finding out what auditory details you get. Think of the experience again.

SOUND

- Do you hear the sound from inside your head or from outside?
- Do you hear it on one side, both sides or is it all around you?
- Is it a voice or some other type of sound?
- Is it loud or soft?
- Is the tonality nasal and whiney or full and rich?
- How full is the sound?
- Where is it coming from?
- How far away is it from you?
- Is it normal speed or faster or slower?
- Is it clear or muffled?
- If it is a voice, is it your voice or someone else's, and if so, whose?
- Does it have rhythm or is it jerky?

What happens when you make pictures and hear sounds is that you get feelings. You may not remember the pictures and sounds and think that you just get the feelings by themselves. Sometimes it does seem like that, but the fact is you don't get feelings on the inside unless you've seen, heard, tasted, smelt or touched something on the outside. Sometimes it happens so quickly that you don't realize what is going on, but internal feelings are chemical reactions to your interpretation of sensory input. Remember the science of emotions? This is what is happening.

So, now let's check out the structure of your feelings. Get back that event and run it through, checking your body.

FEELING

- Where do you feel this experience in your body?
- How would you describe the sensation: tingling, warm, cold, relaxed, tense, knotted, sharp, spread out, bubbly?

- ❤ How strong is the sensation?
- ❤ Is there movement in it?
- ❤ If so, is it continuous or does it come in waves?
- ❤ Where does the feeling start?
- ❤ Where does it leave your body?
- ❤ How did it get from where it started to where it is now? What is its route through your body?
- ❤ Is it slow and steady or does it move in a rush?
- ❤ Is it continuous or intermittent?

Now you have begun to build up a really detailed sense of how you structure your own internal experience. Being aware of this will really help you flirt!

SENSORY LANGUAGE

When I went to the beach with my friend Pammie, the first thing she noticed was the light of the water on the sea. When my friend Stefan visited, he noticed the wind rustling through the trees behind us, the sounds of the gulls and the waves breaking on the shore.

If I were describing the beach to Pammie and Stefan in such a way as to entice them to go there, I'd do it very differently. For Pammie I'd talk about the things she could see. For Stefan I'd describe the sounds.

If you were going to invite someone to a special place or on a date somewhere, how useful would it be to describe it to them using their own language?

You might think that you can't pick up on someone's language in a very short conversation, but the key is to pay attention. If you get someone talking by, for example, asking a question related to the season, you can get quite a lot of information out of them. Don't follow this example as if it were a line, just remember there is always something to make conversation with. If it's summer, say, you could say something like 'Everyone seems to be talking about holidays. What's your favourite holiday destination?' When they answer, you can ask what it is that they like about the destination. In this answer they will probably give you some clues as to how they sense the world. The following lists will give you an idea.

We all use a rich variety of sensory language, but most of us have our preferences and people give you clues to their preferences all the time, through phrases that show they are primarily experiencing their world in terms of vision, sound or feelings. Here are a few examples:

VISION

'Things seem to be blown out of all proportion.'

'This problem is getting on top of me.'

'This task is overwhelming.'

'Life is so dull.'

'I wish I could shed some light on this.'

'You really brightened up my day.'

'I see what you mean.'

'I've got a blind spot about that.'

'I got a flash of inspiration.'

'It was larger than life.'

'It seemed so far away.'

'It's all in your mind's eye.'

'I can't seem to see eye to eye with her.'

'He put her on a pedestal.'

'I just can't see myself doing that.'

'I take a dim view of your activities.'

'Let's take a look at the big picture.'

'I can't seem to get things in perspective.'

SOUND

'We are definitely on the same wavelength.'

'That sounds good to me.'

'I got it loud and clear.'

'Sound like a lot of gibberish.'

'That's all Greek to me.'

'What you said definitely rings a bell with me.'

'I always seem to be dancing to other people's tunes.'

'The answer was screaming out to me.'

'I keep telling myself, "This has got to stop." '

'I want my love life to be more harmonious.'

'I just tuned out the thought of failure.'

'It just kept nagging away at me.'

'That really strikes a chord with me.'

'She turned a deaf ear to his plea.'

'I got it loud and clear.'

TOUCH

'He's a really slimy character.'

'Let's keep in touch.'

'I'm beginning to get to grips with this.'

'I can feel it in my water.'

'It felt as though the weight of the world was on my shoulders.'

'She's very warm-hearted.'

'He's a cold fish.'

'I've got a hot idea.'

'I feel a little off kilter.'

'I'm out of sorts.'

'It's a balancing act.'

'He weighed up the idea.'

'I'm off centre.'

'She had a balanced attitude.'

'She's a really smooth operator.'

'I can't put my finger on it.'

'I'm falling to pieces.'

'I'm pulling myself together.'

'The pressure is on.'

Isn't it amazing how we structure our language in terms of our senses? Best of all, when you are aware of the sensory signals people are sending out, you receive masses of information about how they see the world and you can use that to enhance your communication with them. Remember, good communication is essential for flirting!

So, next time you have a conversation with someone, make a point of keeping your ears open for the type of sensory language they use. A great flirt knows how to make someone feel at home and most of us feel at home when someone talks our language, don't we? You are going to experiment further with developing and using sensory-rich language in Chapter 11.

THE SIGNALS OF FLIRTING

In order to become a superb flirt, it's important to be aware of the signals people send out when they are expressing interest. You need to get two or three clear and repeated signals before you can interpret them as a 'come on'. Here are a few examples of signs that someone is interested in you:

- ❤ accidentally brushing up against you
- ❤ nodding their head whilst looking in your direction
- ❤ pointing to a chair and inviting you to sit down
- ❤ smiling broadly at you
- ❤ throwing a short darting glance in your direction
- ❤ batting their eyelashes and looking up and sideways
- ❤ beckoning with their head or hands or sideways tilted head
- ❤ complimenting you

- flaring their nostrils
- dilating their pupils
- thrusting out their chest or breasts
- blowing out a match and holding it whilst looking at you
- playing with their tie or jewellery
- winking at you
- raising an eyebrow

On the other hand, here are some signals that indicate that someone is not interested:

- brief eye contact
- looking away quickly
- keeping the same posture
- turning their body away from you
- keeping their head vertical
- normal or dull eyes
- a closed mouth
- sagging so as not to emphasize their breasts/chest
- looking at someone else lustily!

KEEP PLAYING WITH IT

Of course you'll need to have sharp senses to pick these clues up! So, as a parting thought, I ask you to play with this little exploration:

- Next time you start to feel bad about something, stop and ask yourself: 'How am I doing this?'
- Start to become aware of the things you say to yourself and the kind of voices you use.
- Notice which images are useful and not so useful.
- Check whether you are in the experience (associated) or watching yourself in it (dissociated).

Just being aware of your own and other people's sensory output will enable you to make changes that will improve the way you communicate. We'll work on this in more detail later. First it's time to work out what you are like at your very best!

CHAPTER 4

BEING YOUR *best you*

'To be what we are, and to become what we are capable of becoming, is the only end of life.'

Robert Louis Stevenson

SIMPLY THE BEST

Flirting comes from being yourself at your best, loving yourself and giving out the glow of who you are.

What's true of you when you are at your best, completely and utterly?

You do know. Because at some time you have experienced those magical moments. In fact you are going to discover that you already have a full body memory of being like that. It's just waiting to be reactivated!

This chapter is derived from the work of my mentor Joseph Riggio and the MythoSelf™ process.

THE SLIVER OF SPACE THAT IS YOU

There is a sliver of space that is you and when you are there, living in it, everything works just fine. You realize that anything is possible. You have a sense of how your life can be and you begin to work towards some kind of intent that is larger than you but really you. When problems crop up, you just say, 'What's next? What can I learn from this?' and move on. Like this, you can flirt like an angel or a devil, if that is what is inside you, because you are being true to who you are. People love it and you do too. Every juicy minute of it. So, how do you find it?

PETA'S STORY:
How I Found My Sliver of Space

A few years ago, I was going through some challenges in my personal life. For a long time I was working on temporary secretarial assignments. I resented and hated this work, but thought that I had to do it, that I didn't have a choice. It seemed as though I was constantly battling life. It wasn't fair. I didn't know what I wanted. All I knew was what I didn't want. I did a lot of wild and crazy things. I was suppressing my true nature, lacked belief in myself and was afraid to move. I was stuck. Do you know the feeling?

For three years a friend who runs a financial health seminar had been trying to enrol me on the course. I wasn't interested. Then one day, as I was clearing some papers on my desk, I found my friend's brochure. The course was starting the next day. For some reason, I just called and enrolled. It seemed like the right thing to do and I didn't know why until the middle of the first day when the co-facilitator, Joseph Riggio, started to talk to us. I was sitting back, just drifting along, and suddenly I heard some words that made me sit up and really listen:

When you stand in that sliver of space that is completely and utterly you, that's when you are truly wonderful, splendid, abundant!

I gasped. I felt a tingle go through my body and for a moment I actually experienced that feeling of being in a sliver of space, being myself. Those words had sent me immediately into a body memory of being myself at my best. It was wonderful. '*This* is what I want,' I said to myself. One sentence and I knew why I had come on the course. And it wasn't to sort out my finances!

MARIE'S STORY:
A Changed Life

When you get in touch with yourself at your best, amazing things can happen. Thirty-seven and single, Marie enrolled on a flirting weekend because she wanted to find a partner. She was a business contacts manager and everyone said she had a good job, but she hated it. She thought finding a partner would make her feel happier, but she got a lot more than she bargained for! Let her tell you in her own words:

As a result of getting in touch with myself at my best, I achieved my goal last week of getting accepted for an MBA at a prestigious business management college. When I first considered this two years ago I could only come up with a list of reasons why not – I didn't have a great first degree, I was too old, other people would get places before me, I couldn't finance it . . . Instead of trying for it, I gave up and I moved into a job I knew I could do.

And now I look forward to resigning from my job in the next few months.

I'm also experiencing wonders in another area of my life – I am now dating a great guy who loves me for what I am, not what he hopes I might become.

YOUR REAL YOU IS THERE...

You cannot be given a life by someone else. Of all the people you will know in a lifetime, you are the only one you will never leave or lose. To the question of your life, you are the only answer. To the problems of your life, you are the only solution.

Jo Coudert

The real you, your best self, is there for you. It has been quietly and sometimes not so quietly trying to get you to set it free. I bet it's given you some signals over the years. Perhaps you've experienced something like this:

- ❤ a voice that nags you or cajoles you to listen out for more
- ❤ a vision of something just out of reach that sometimes appears and then disappears
- ❤ a persistent feeling that something isn't right
- ❤ something you heard or read somewhere that made you think, 'Is there more out there?'

You may have received these signals – and ignored them. Before I heard those sliver of space words, I had already had several wake-up calls myself. If you are like me, it may take more than one call to get you into action and you will get there when *you* are ready. My first one was from Barbara Sher's book *Wishcraft*. These words shone out at me when I first read them:

If a seed is given good soil and plenty of water and sun, it doesn't have to try to unfold, it doesn't need self-confidence or self-discipline or perseverance. It just unfolds. It can't help unfolding.

If a seed has to grow with a rock on top of it, or in deep shade or without enough water, it won't unfold into a healthy sized plant. It will try – hard – because the drive to become what you are meant to be is incredibly powerful. But at its best it will become a sort of ghost of what it could be. In a way, that's what most of us are.

Do you feel that you are a 'sort of ghost' of what you could be? Don't worry. When you find out how you are at your absolute best and begin to be like that more and more, you open out like that seed to embrace the sun, the rain and the earth's nurture. You begin to have a sense of how you want your life to be. You attract the situations and people that are right for you. You flirt like crazy!

My great mistake, the fault for which I can't forgive myself, is that one day I ceased my obstinate pursuit of my individuality.

Oscar Wilde

HOW TO ACCESS YOUR BEST SELF

How do you do it? It's simple. If you want it you can have it as long as you are prepared to stick with it, follow the directions and go for it. This is how it works:

You check out how you are right now.
You decide you want to be your best self.
You begin to recall experiences of being yourself at your best.
As you do this, you notice what is happening in your body – your posture, movement, breathing, balance.
You become aware of the images you are making in your mind's eye and what you are saying in your head.
You come up with a word that describes this state perfectly.
You choose a symbol which represents this state.
You use all this information to be your best self more and more.
Life gets sweeter!

I've devised some explorations to help you. Let's start with where you are now.

WHERE ARE YOU RIGHT NOW?

This is where you get to ask yourself some questions and give back some home truths. All I ask is that you are honest with yourself, recognize what you are doing and focus on the possibilities and alternatives. When that happens, you will begin to glow more and you will just feel more flirtatious!

Think about the following questions. You don't have to write down your thoughts, although it may help you to clarify them.

On a scale of 1–10, where 1 is 'very little' and 10 is 'yes, absolutely!', rate how much you are really yourself:

- in your work
- with your workmates
- with friends
- with family
- when you meet new people
- with a partner if you have one

What masks are you wearing? What are you doing that is not you? How would you like to be?

- Do you want to be more fulfilled at work or do you want to be doing a completely different job, maybe something you have secretly yearned to do?
- Do you want to live out some dreams that you have not dared realize?
- Do you want to have a wonderful relationship?

I wonder what's been stopping you. Is there something you are doing that is preventing you from being your best self? What do you want to stop doing? What do you want to be doing?

To give you an idea, Marie wanted to stop underrating herself, finding excuses for not doing things and being so negative. She wanted to love herself more, believe in herself, take risks and be happy.

Now it's your turn:

I want to stop doing:

I want to be/do:

Great. Congratulate yourself for doing that exploration. You've taken a giant leap forward.

Now you are ready for the next stage!

HOW'S YOUR RELATIONSHIP WITH YOURSELF?

You know that before you can flirt with life, you have to flirt with yourself. In this next exploration I invite you to evaluate your relationship with yourself. And from there you can move onwards and upwards towards SuccessFlirtdom!

YOUR RELATIONSHIP WITH YOURSELF

Again, you can answer these questions in your head or write down your thoughts in your notebook.

- ♥ Are you listening to your real self? (Do you sometimes get urges to behave differently or try new things or just go a little wild and stop yourself by saying you can't or you shouldn't or you ought not to?)
- ♥ Do you believe anything is possible for you?
- ♥ Are you allowing yourself free expression of who you are?
- ♥ Are you pampering yourself and speaking encouragingly to yourself?
- ♥ Do you congratulate yourself when you do something well?
- ♥ Are you happy to talk about your good points?
- ♥ Do you believe that to take care of others you must take care of yourself first?
- ♥ Do you think that you, like everyone, are special and unique?

Did you answer 'yes' to all of those? Yes? Congratulations! Continue to do more of it. No? Great! Read on!

YOUR BODY IS THE KEY

Now I'm going to ask you some questions that will bring to mind thoughts of you at your best. In answering these, it's important to pay attention to your body. The reason for this is that to bring back your 'you at your best' way of being is to 'remember' it in your mind *and* your body! So before you answer the questions, let's look at just how important body awareness is.

We get far more from tone of voice and body language than from the actual meaning of the words.

You can pick up these signals from other people, but more importantly, you can pick them up from yourself. Finding out how your body responds to a stimulus is a major route to discovering the physical configuration of yourself at your best. Once you discover this, it's much easier for you to practise getting back there more and more. Then you will actually notice positive changes in your thinking and how you feel about yourself.

WHAT'S YOUR RHYTHM?

We all have a body rhythm – our heart beats rhythmically, we have a pulse that changes and we walk with our own rhythm. We have rhythms that disturb us and rhythms that soothe and motivate us.

My friend Billy told me how when he was a child he always felt really peaceful and calm when he sat watching his grandmother sew on a machine. The rhythm of the machine's sounds seemed to hypnotize him.

What rhythms affect you? If you listen to music, is there anything special you like to exercise to, make love to, relax to? Do you play an instrument? Do you, like Billy, remember a special rhythm from your childhood? You can find your own rhythm. Tom did.

TOM'S STORY: *Drumming into Life*

Tom had come to me because he wanted to be more confident when he talked to girls. I asked him the magic question: 'What do you know to be true about yourself when you're at your best – absolutely? What are you doing when you are like that?'

Tom uncrossed his knees and started to talk about playing the drums, how he had rhythm and could become one with the beat. He started to tap his hands rhythmically on his knees.

I encouraged him to keep his rhythm, snapping my fingers in time to his own beat. He sat up and adjusted his shoulders and his breathing changed. As he sat there, he slowed down the tapping and began to rock to the same rhythm with his whole body. He was himself at his best and he had got into that state through a rhythm that resonated with him.

'So,' I asked, 'what would it be like talking to someone new when you are like this, with rhythm, in synch with the beat of that person?'

His mouth opened, but he didn't speak.

I said, 'Like this, what is possible?'

He answered, 'Anything,' and smiled.

Tom had accessed a full rhythmic body memory of being in his sliver of space and as a result he became aware of a world full of possibilities.

HOW SHARP IS YOUR BODY AWARENESS?

When you do this exploration, you will increase your body awareness quite considerably.

As you read through the following list, be aware of what you notice in your body. Make a note of it later, if you wish.

- Sit up straight. Start to breathe evenly. If you need to, uncross your legs or ankles.
- Feel your head on your neck. Is it stiff or is it loose and lightly balanced? Adjust it.
- What sensations and changes are you noticing elsewhere in your body?
- Are your hands tense or are they fairly relaxed, even if they are holding this book?
- How are your shoulders? Are they hunched against your neck or are they just resting naturally, drawn down by gravity?
- What of your back, is it comfortable, and if not, can you adjust it to make it so?
- What happens when you vary, very slowly, your line of sight? If you are looking down to your right, try looking up and, with your head straight ahead, move your eyes very slowly to the left and then the right, stopping to notice the effects on your body as you do so.

Now check your body from toe to head:

- Focus on the area from your feet to the tops of your legs and a little higher. What do you notice?
- Focus on the area just below your navel. What do you notice?
- Move your focus up slowly to your solar plexus. What do you notice?
- Check out your heart area. How does this feel?
- Move up to your throat, noticing the different sensations.
- Then focus on your forehead. What do you notice when you do that?
- Now shift your attention to the top of your head. How does that feel?

- If you were sitting with your knees or ankles crossed, what happens if you uncross them? Notice the difference.
- Try uncrossing and crossing your legs.
- Try opening out your legs wider. What does that feel like?
- If you can and are not already doing so, stand up and spread your feet about a foot. Put your hands on your hips and look straight ahead. Breathe evenly and deeply but gently in and out. Keep your head straight ahead, and survey the scene.
- Shift your shoulders down and as you breathe in, expand your chest as if pulling back your arms a little. Smile, even if it means putting on a smile to start with. What do you notice?
- How do you normally stand and how do you stand when you are feeling good?
- Is there any rhythm that comes to mind? You can move in time to it. What difference does that make? This is something you can learn to do more and more – if you want to!

DISCOVERING YOUR BEST SELF

This exploration is designed to help you access your best self, so negatives are forbidden. If at any time during it you think of what you *don't* like, change it to what you *do* like.

Take some time and get comfortable. You can write down the answers to the questions as you ask them or you can try answering the questions out loud in front of a mirror. This has two purposes:

1 You can not only feel but also see what you are doing as you answer.
2 You say something out loud, which is a way of affirming it is true.

If this feels a bit silly, great. When you do so-called 'silly' things like talking to yourself or bursting out laughing in public or jumping in puddles, you are actually giving yourself age-regression therapy, taking years off your age by boosting your immune system and freeing yourself from unspoken, unowned rules that limit and hold you back!

To answer the questions out loud, stand in front of the mirror, ask yourself the questions in your head and reply out loud. Adjust yourself until you feel right. You can do this as often as you need in order to feel more like your best self!

Whatever comes up is OK.

Question	Your reactions to the question, thoughts, images, feelings	Your answer	What is happening in your body now?
What did you love to do as a child?			
What sense did you live most through or did you live through them equally? Did you see things, make images, did you talk a lot to yourself, were you more aware of sounds, did you just feel things . . . Describe it			
What are your greatest achievements? These can be as simple as growing a plant to founding your own empire . . . What have you done that you looked back and thought . . . that was lovely, that was me . . .			
What skills, talents, abilities, shine out in you?			
What things do you have a real passion for?			
What do you like best about yourself?			
What 3 positive adjectives would you use to describe yourself quickly off the top of your head?			
What are your fondest memories of being you?			
What are your fondest memories of having fun?			
What is true of you that you would like people to remember about you when you are dead?			
What do you know to be true about you when you're at your best – absolutely?			
How do you know?			

FLIRT COACH

Be yourself. The world worships the original.

Ingrid Bergman

TRIGGERING A GOOD FEELING

You've probably heard of Pavlov's dogs. Pavlov was experimenting with autonomic or trigger response. He fed the dogs and as they salivated and enjoyed the food, he rang the bell. After a few times, the dogs linked the experience of eating to the sound of the bell. Pavlov could just ring the bell and the dogs salivated. He had created a trigger for the full body memory of the delicious anticipation of food. . .

Like Pavlov's dogs, we react to triggers. When these triggers are fired, they bring back the experience they are linked to. A song is a perfect example. Years later just a few notes of music may be enough to send you right back into a special moment.

The strongest triggers are the ones that coincide with the peak of a feeling, whether bad or good. When this happens naturally the trigger is often out of your control. But you can learn to activate your own triggers. How much easier would it be to feel your best self if you could activate a trigger to put you in that state? You might use a word to describe it.

SARAH'S STORY: *Carefree*

When I asked Sarah what word came to mind to describe her at her best she said, 'Carefree.' This word is a symbol for all the molecules of emotion that make up what she feels in her body when she is at her best. Each time Sarah thinks of the word 'carefree' and says it the way she said it when I asked her, it brings her back to the physical sense of how she is at her best.

A NATURAL SYMBOL

Alternatively, you might prefer to use a symbol as well as or instead of a word. One of the most potent symbols is that of an animal. Throughout history, in various cultures, animals have been used to represent certain qualities. A lion is often associated with courage, for example, whilst a squirrel is associated with being busy and getting things done and an eagle is associated with looking down on the world and getting a clear view from an 'eagle eye'. Many charming books have been written about the symbolism of animals. We are all familiar with a wide range of animals and if you think about an animal I am sure you will easily be able to associate it with some quality.

When participants in my flirting class do this exploration, they are often surprised by the animals or symbols that come to mind when they think of how they are at their best. To give you an idea of what I mean, here are Paul, Jenny and Rob's stories.

PAUL, JENNY AND ROB'S STORIES:
The Lion, the Sun and the Chimpanzee

Paul wanted to be more sexually attractive. As he began to access what was true of himself at his best, I asked him what animal came to mind as a symbol of how he was. He didn't take long to think of a lion. When I asked him what had made him pick the lion, he said, 'Because it is ferocious and bold.' These were qualities he wanted to access.

Jenny wanted to socialize more. She couldn't decide on an animal as a symbol of how she felt at her best and finally picked the sun, as she said being her socializing best was about 'shining so that other people feel warm in my presence'.

Rob was quite a serious man and wanted to loosen up. He decided the symbol of how he wanted to be was a chimpanzee. When I asked him what made him choose a chimp, he said, 'Because I'm running around and having fun.' It worked for him!

How about you?

FINDING YOUR ANIMAL SYMBOL

Read these instructions first and then find somewhere quiet where you will not be disturbed.

Access again how you are when you are at your best, absolutely. Close your eyes, get a full body sense of it. Remember the word that came to mind as you did this before and ask yourself these questions:

♥   What animal, real or mythical, symbolizes how I am at my best, absolutely?

Let whatever animal appears first come up and then ask yourself:

♥   What is it about this animal that symbolizes how I am at my best?

People are often surprised at the animal or symbol that comes to mind. Some people think they ought to have a glamorous symbol or animal. *Not true.* Once when I was looking for a symbol – and I do it often – I came up with an elephant. When I looked up the symbolic meaning attached to elephants I realized why. It symbolizes being part of a society, libido and great strength. I was in the process of connecting to a new community after moving home and I was doing research for a book on sex and enjoying my own sex life in the process and the tree at the bottom of my garden always reminded me of an elephant's leg! I didn't know about the ancient symbolism of the elephant and yet it was perfect for me. Sometimes our mind just does things that are absolutely right for us when we let it have free rein.

Each animal, large or small, has its own uniquely wonderful qualities. Life is about the beauty within and the perception of beauty which exists in every one of us.

GETTING THE MOST FROM YOUR SYMBOL

Remember that the animal symbol that comes up for you is symbolic of some of the qualities you have now. You may find that your symbol changes later as you change too. That's fine. But for now let's concentrate on the one that has come up for you.

- Once your animal symbol comes to mind, begin to research it. Find out all you can about it.
- If you use a computer, use a picture of your animal as wallpaper or as a screensaver.
- Cut out pictures of your animal and stick them in places where you spend time – on your desk, beside your bed, wherever it will be most appropriate for you to remember all that this animal symbolizes.
- Keep some symbol of the animal near you – maybe even a stone that makes you think of it.
- Spend some time imagining how your animal moves.
- What does its way of moving say about you?
- Watch nature programmes about your animal.
- Familiarize yourself with its unique abilities.

What does your animal embody in you?

This is adapted from the work of Ted Andrews.

Animals have something to teach us all. They are constantly interacting either with their own species or different animals or humans. Take the lioness chasing the gazelle, the way she stalks, waits, alert, silent. Look at the way birds swoop down on things with an eye for detail in the middle of a big picture. Notice how a butterfly hovers from flower to flower and remains just out of reach.

So how flirtatious would you be if you were patient, independent, moved endearingly, had an eye for detail, were alert and open to new people?

The qualities you find in your animal are qualities you are looking to access more in yourself.

SENSING YOUR ANIMAL

First read through the instructions and then find somewhere quiet to do this exploration.

- Pinpoint two or three major qualities of your animal.
- Take a few moments to relax and think back over your life, starting from now, in five-year increments. Try to determine times in your life when you exhibited those same qualities.
- When you find those moments, make a mental picture of the animal and note how good you feel and where in your body you have the feeling.
- Also see those times in your life when you would have benefited from exhibiting those qualities, but didn't. How might they have helped you?
- Think of a time in the future, perhaps a job interview, an encounter with someone, a relationship issue, and imagine how exhibiting those qualities might help you experience this situation more richly.

Remember that flirting is not just about the superficial outward displays, but about what is going on inside you. Flirting starts with who you are shining through. So it is important that you have some way of accessing your best self, easily and quickly. When you trigger this, through your animal or word or in some other way, you will find this is the perfect state of mind in which to flirt and attract others to you.

And remembering how wonderful it is to discover how you are at your best, it is also important to believe that it is possible to be like this. Sometimes we block what is possible by taking on beliefs that stop us from letting loose the wonderful flirtatious person inside. The next chapter is designed to help you free yourself from beliefs that limit you so that you can begin to enjoy yourself at your best even more.

CHAPTER 5

BUILDING BETTER *beliefs*

To accomplish great things, we must not only act but also dream, not only plan but believe.

Anatole France

WOULD YOU BELIEVE IT?

A group of frogs was travelling through the woods and two of them fell into a deep pit. All the other frogs gathered around the pit. When they saw how deep it was, they told the two frogs that they were as good as dead.

At first both frogs ignored the comments and tried to jump up out of the pit with all of their might.

Finally, one of the frogs took heed of what the other frogs were saying and gave up. He fell down and died . . .

What happened to the other frog?

BELIEFS: OUR DRIVING FORCE

Beliefs have the power to create and the power to destroy.

Tony Robbins

What we believe is the driving force behind what we do. Some people are driven by positive, motivating, useful, energizing beliefs. They believe things like:

- I'm a winner.
- Whatever happens, it will all work out OK.
- Everything happens for a reason.
- I'm desirable.

Successful athletes are driven by similar beliefs. They believe totally and utterly they are winners. They mentally rehearse themselves winning. They say motivational words to themselves. They praise themselves when they do well. They *believe* they are winners.

When you adopt empowering beliefs, your life will begin to move in the direction of your dreams and desires. Your beliefs are your support and motivation.

EMPOWERING BELIEFS: FERTILE EARTH

Empowering beliefs nourish, revive and enrich you like fertile earth. They are like sweet music to your ears and they shine light on whatever you do.

Great flirts live by empowering beliefs. They believe they are desirable. They believe they are sexy. They believe they bring a little light into other people's lives and they believe other people are interesting.

LIMITING BELIEFS: STONY GROUND

Some beliefs can have a very limiting and weakening effect on you. For example, if you believe you are not attractive, you will act as if you are not and you'll probably look less attractive to others. If you believe you won't have anything to say at a party, you'll probably find yourself drying up even though everyone has something to talk about! If you believe that you'll blow an approach to someone, chances are you will. What you believe sets you up to act accordingly. It's a self-fulfilling prophecy – although there are times when you don't believe you can do something and you surprise yourself. But often when this happens people pass it off as a fluke! Limiting beliefs are like stony ground. They don't allow you to grow and flourish because they are toxic.

BELIEFS ARE JUST STORIES

Beliefs, like jokes, are just stories. Unfortunately, many jokes perpetrate certain toxic beliefs. Take this one:

Men are like a fine wine. They start out like grapes and it's our job to stomp on them and keep them in the dark until they mature into something you'd like to have dinner with.

We laugh at this stuff, yet we are buying into a particular belief system when we do so. How many women do you know who believe men should be trained and changed to fit the mould?

THE HISTORY OF BELIEFS

The reason you have problems is because you were born, had parents and went to school.

Richard Bandler

Where did your beliefs come from? From birth until about the age of two, you exist in a state of innocence and wonder, acting with your natural instincts of curiosity, playfulness and derring-do! You believe that anything is possible.

After the age of three, slowly but surely you begin to absorb other people's beliefs, both good and bad. Children are like sponges, they don't differentiate, they just take everything in – and so do some adults!

Just take a moment to compare baby beliefs with adult beliefs.

BABIES COULD EASILY THINK:

BABIES COULD EASILY THINK:	**ADULTS OFTEN THINK:**

'I'm hungry.' — 'Don't be greedy.'

'I want attention.' — 'Stop being so demanding.'

'I need love.' — 'Why would anyone want to love me?'

'I am exploring. I am reaching out.' — 'Don't touch. It's rude to touch. Don't touch yourself there.'

'I am the centre of my world.' — 'Who do you think you are?'

'When I see someone, I'll smile at them.' — 'It's not done to smile at strangers, they might think you are crazy.'

'When I meet someone, I'll communicate.' — 'Perhaps they won't want to talk to me.'

'I can see someone's eyes. I'll look in them.' — 'Don't look, they might know I like them. They might see through me if I look them in the eye.'

'If I fall down, I get up.' — 'Oh no, I've failed. There's no point in trying again, I'll only fail again.'

'If I want something, I'll go for it.' — 'I'll never be able to do that, I'm no good. You can't have it all.'

'If I try something one way and it doesn't work, I'll try it another way.' — 'An old dog can't learn new tricks.'

'Gurgle, gurgle – this is such fun!' — 'Fun is for kids!'

Which beliefs would you rather have?

CHANGING BELIEFS

The greatest revelation of our time is the discovery that human beings, by changing the inner attitudes of their minds, can change the outer aspects of their lives.

William James

If you feel you are driven by some limiting beliefs, take heart. You can change those beliefs. You've already done it! You used to believe things at one time that you no longer believe now. You may have believed in Santa Claus or the Tooth Fairy once. Do you believe in them now?

'TEACHER TOLD ME SO IT MUST BE TRUE'

Denis Waitley, a psychologist, tells the story of an experiment scientists did with the belief systems of children. Teachers were asked to tell their pupils that all the brown-eyed eight year olds were more intelligent than the blue-eyed kids. In a test shortly after, the brown-eyed students soared ahead of the blue-eyed ones. Even those blue-eyed students who had previously done well performed poorly.

The teachers then told the students that they had made a mistake and that in fact blue-eyed students were more intelligent than brown-eyed ones. In the next test, the blue-eyed students came out on top. Even those brown-eyed students who had done well before got lower marks.

These kids changed their beliefs in themselves because they had a stronger belief: *Teacher is always right!*

When you were growing up you may have heard adults say things that became your beliefs. These may be empowering or limiting you now. Hilary and Sue, for example, heard very different stories about their freckles.

HILARY'S AND SUE'S STORIES:
'Freckles Are...'

Hilary believes she will never be beautiful because she has freckles. She always wears thick pancake make up to hide them. Sue loves her freckles, is well aware that they keep her looking young and thinks that they are sexy. She never wears face make up. What's the difference between these two?

Long ago Hilary's mother told her, 'You are pretty, Hilary, but you will never be beautiful because you have freckles.'

Long ago Sue's father used to hug her and call her 'my beautiful little freckled princess'. He told her that each freckle meant she had been blessed by angels, which meant her life would be happier and more fun than those of people without freckles!

Both Hilary and Sue took on their parents' stories and it affected their beliefs about their own beauty.

Are there toxic stories that you have turned into truths? Are they limiting you? When I received this book back from the editor she suggested that beliefs need to be believable, using the example that she was so bad at maths that there was no way in the world she'd be good at it! This is exactly what prevents people from progressing. Early on they've had a bad experience and someone in authority has installed and reinforced a belief that they will never be able to do something. We are all able to be good at maths, some people just need a different type of teaching.

Richard was worried about being able to do the written exercises on my flirting course. He said, 'I won't have to read anything out loud, will I?' When he was at school, he was abysmal at spelling. The teacher used to make him write up his work on the board and read it out to the class. It was supposed to be an English class but perhaps it should be renamed Humiliation 101!

Naturally there are some limitations on what we can all do. I don't expect to be courted by Brad Pitt even though I might like to dream about it. When I think about it realistically, it isn't right for me! Sometimes there are physical limitations. If you believe you are too old to realize a dream of becoming a big sports star, maybe you are, but perhaps you could help some kid to realize their sporting dream . . . Not a bad substitute, is it?

So, just for a moment, take some time to forget all the stories you've been told about what you can't do and allow your dreams of what you'd like to be able to do take over. I am sure you can come up with some juicy things you'd like to believe about yourself. Now's your chance.

The following explorations offer useful tools for exchanging your limiting beliefs for more useful ones.

BEING YOUR BELIEF

I'm sure you have some juicy beliefs you'd like to believe about yourself. Now's your chance to create them and embody them.

- Think of a belief you want to have about yourself.
- Create a sentence that affirms that belief. Start with either of these two phrases:

    I can. . .
    I am. . .

- Now say to yourself: 'When I am at my best, I can/am [your belief].'
- Now think of someone who has that belief about themselves or acts as if they believe something similar about themselves. For example, if you want to be more raunchy, Tina Turner might be a good role model.
- Pay attention to how your role model stands, moves, breathes and acts.
- Stand like that yourself.
- Say the belief to yourself over and over in your head.
- How are you breathing with this new belief?
- How are you holding your head with this new belief?
- Where are you looking with this new belief?
- Say your new belief out loud.
- Continue to stand there for a while with the body stance of this new belief.

The more you do this, the more your body takes on the cell memories of the belief and the more it appears as if it is true. Then one day it just is!

CHIPPING AWAY AT USELESS BELIEFS

Over the years you have absorbed and unconsciously created beliefs and if you don't want them you can ditch them. No one says they are the law! Of course we aren't talking about things like believing it is wrong to steal – these are beliefs that were put in place to maintain social harmony. I am talking about some of the beliefs you have about yourself that prevent you from being flirtatious, charismatic and going out and having all the fun you deserve. Ask yourself if these beliefs are serving you.

If other people try to tell you something that doesn't make you feel good, you can either simply reject it or work out whether there's anything valuable in it – and that might make you feel good! I was talking to a friend about an idea for a new book and she reminded me that there were probably a few in progress right now on the same subject. This didn't stop me believing I could do it, but it did encourage me to become more creative in what I wanted to do.

QUESTIONING BELIEFS

When you start to question a belief it begins to weaken.

If you feel you have some limiting beliefs that are holding you back, take heart, you can crack them open and step out of them. A good start is to really question the validity of the beliefs and rules you live by.

Make a list of some things you believe and write them down. Look at each one and ask yourself:

- Does this belief or rule help me to be who I am or not?
- Is believing this helping me to fulfil my dreams in any way?
- Does believing this make me feel good about myself?
  If the answer is 'yes', keep affirming the belief and ignore any criticism or comments.
  If the answer is 'no', well done! You know what you have to crack open!

REJECTION AND FAILURE: DEMOLITION DERBY

All my successes have been built on my failures.

Benjamin Disraeli

Some very common beliefs are that you will fail or be rejected. But what is failure exactly? Failure is just a result. It might not be the result you want, but it's not an ending, it's a beginning.

People often say things like 'I've got a history of rejection.' The belief that your history of rejection is going to determine your future is another very limiting belief.

Rejection is just someone making a decision about what is right for them.

When you can think of failure and rejection as useful tools to help you improve, it's like learning to walk — you keep trying and eventually you get the result.

If what you are doing isn't working, *try something else.*

He was so bad that he was cut from his high school basketball team.

He said, 'I have missed more than 9,000 shots in my career. I have lost almost 300 games. On 26 occasions I have been entrusted to take the game-winning shot . . . and missed. And I have failed over and over and over again in my life.'

Quite a failure, huh?!

And lastly he said, 'And that is precisely . . . why I succeed.'

Who said this? Michael Jordan, one of the world's best basketball players ever.

NO, NEXT!

One of the things I advise all my students is that 'no' can be a signal to either try a different approach or move on to something else. I am constantly reminding them: 'When you get a "no", go on to the next. *No, next, no, next! Bingo! Yes!*'

Hamdi, one of my students, took this to heart. He learned to say 'no' to rejection and see the *next* opportunity coming in. Here's how he described his progress:

When you said, '*No, next*', I assumed the girls would be saying the 'no' and I'd be accepting it! But once I started believing that rejection was a learning, things started to change. Recently it has been me saying 'no'. I never thought that day would come. And as time goes on I am meeting more women and the level of connection is deeper and soon I will meet one with whom I can develop a *Bingo!*

You see, it's all a matter of how you look at it and whether you allow events to infect or, like Hamdi, inspire your life. Great flirts often get a 'no', but they don't care, they just act differently or move on to someone else.

TURNING LIMITING BELIEFS AROUND

To inspire you further, here are some of the great beliefs that people in my flirting workshops created to replace their limiting beliefs.

LIMITING BELIEF	EMPOWERING NEW BELIEF
I am too old for the men you meet in pubs and clubs.	There are loads of other places to meet people. I'm open to new ideas.
I'm too old.	My age is a sign of my wisdom.
	I love telling people how old I am because they are always surprised at how young I appear.
I'm afraid of failure.	Failure teaches me more.
	I like failure, because it means I'm closer to winning.
If I meet someone, we might not be compatible.	I'd hate to be with someone who doesn't like me!
I'm shy.	My life's a party and I'm the host! Saying 'hello' is like handing out the canapés.
He will let me down/be an awful lover/stop being considerate.	When I am at my best I will attract a loyal, sexy, loving and considerate man.
Men are vulnerable. My dad used to say a man chases a woman until she catches him.	Women are chasing me and I am choosing whether to accept or not.

The other person will not find me interesting.

Not everyone will like me and that's OK. Someone out there will like me.

Men like blonde bimbos.

Men love me because I am dark and mysterious looking.

As you become more aware of which beliefs limit you, you are closer to changing them. One question I ask participants in my flirting classes is: *'What stops you from flirting or connecting with or enjoying conversations with other people?'*

What is your answer? Does it bring forth a host of limiting beliefs? Would you like to banish them?

BANISHING BELIEFS THAT LIMITED YOU

Write down your limiting beliefs, using these opening phrases:

- 💜 I was. . .
- 💜 I used to. . .
- 💜 I didn't have. . .
- 💜 I couldn't. . .

For example:

- 💜 I was afraid of rejection.
- 💜 I used to think I was too fat.
- 💜 I didn't have any confidence.
- 💜 I couldn't think of what to say.

Using the past tense tricks your brain into starting to think of those beliefs as past!

Then ask yourself:

- ❤ What did this belief do for me?
- ❤ How did it stop me?
- ❤ What's wrong with this belief?
- ❤ What emotional mess did I pile up for myself by believing this?

Now, look carefully at your list and become aware of the disservice these beliefs have done you.

Stop! That's enough pain. The point here is not to live in the past and wallow in pain, but to move on and ask, 'What is next?'

WELCOME IN NEW EMPOWERING BELIEFS

In this exploration you are going to create some amazing new beliefs for yourself.

Find somewhere quiet to do this. Take a piece of paper and divide it up into two columns. In the left column write your old belief *in the past tense*. Ask yourself:

What new, more empowering belief do I want in its place?

When you become aware of a new empowering belief, write it down in the second column opposite the old belief.

Ask yourself:

What will be the benefits of this new belief and how will it empower me?

For example:

OLD BELIEF	NEW BELIEF	BENEFITS OF THE NEW BELIEF
I used to believe I was fat.	I'm cuddly and voluptuous.	I feel better about myself and more people will be attracted to me.

By participating in this exploration, you have begun to create new ideas for yourself. Continue to do this every time you become aware of a belief that limits you.

Now we're going to spend some time locking in your new empowering beliefs.

TALKING YOURSELF INTO NEW BELIEFS

Some years ago, I realized I was stuck. I was limiting myself by my lack of self-belief and the fact that I was scared to change and I felt very unfulfilled. I devised a set of positive beliefs based on the opposite of what I actually believed at the time. My belief list read:

- ❤ I am believing in myself.
- ❤ I am taking risks.
- ❤ I am at peace.

Even though I didn't really believe these words, I wanted to. I repeated them daily until it became natural to have this voice running through my head saying great things. I said them all the time. I spoke life into these beliefs. The more you say what you want to believe, the more it appears to be true.

I wonder what beliefs you'd like to create and affirm for yourself?

'IMPOSSIBLE BELIEFS' ARE POSSIBILITIES!

'There is no use trying,' said Alice; 'one can't believe impossible things.' 'I dare say you haven't had much practice,' said the Queen. 'When I was your age, I always did it for half an hour a day. Why, sometimes I've believed as many as six impossible things before breakfast.'

Lewis Carroll

What kind of so-called 'impossible' things would be great to believe about yourself? Make sure that they are things that don't depend on others, like believing you can marry Brad Pitt. But even as I write that, I am mindful of the woman who decided she was going to marry her pop idol, Gary Numan, and she did! So perhaps what might seem impossible isn't really!

With that in mind, though, it might be more useful to concentrate on things that you want to believe about your career and your ability to attract friends and the right partner into your life.

BELIEVING IN YOUR FUTURE

- ❤ Write down 10 empowering things you want to believe about yourself in the future.
- ❤ Look at the 10 things you have written in turn. Stop as you look silently and check your feelings about each one in turn.
- ❤ Which one do you want the most? Which next? Your feelings are your guide.
- ❤ Prioritize them in order.

DRAW ON YOUR BELIEFS

If you feel inclined, you can sit down with a piece of blank paper and draw out or design your beliefs.

If you want to, use coloured pens and draw symbols. You can type up your beliefs on a computer, add graphic art, change the font and hang them in a frame on the wall. One friend had them on pieces of coloured card, swinging from a mobile. Another person I know has her affirmation beliefs as a screensaver! How about recording them on to tape?

What wonderful reminders can you create that will help you affirm those great new beliefs?

A TAILORED BELIEF CHANGE

When you think of something you really believe in and something you want to believe but don't yet, how do you experience them in your body? What's the difference?

When you really believe something it may be like seeing a movie and feeling as if you are the centre of it. It might be what you hear or say to yourself that spurs you on or it might be that final feeling that really tells you you are on track. Sometimes it's a combination of all three.

When you really believe something empowering, it will have a specific combination of sounds, images and feelings – a template for this type of belief.

STRUCTURING NEW BELIEFS

This exploration is about adjusting how you structure beliefs you want to be true by reformatting them to fit the structural template you use when you experience beliefs that you do believe to be true.

To do this you need the 'structure of experience' lists on pp. 33–35 and possibly something to write with.

- ❤ Find a quiet space where you won't be disturbed and relax.
- ❤ Mark out a spot you can move to and call it 'true belief' spot.
- ❤ Mark out another spot and call it 'want to believe' spot.
- ❤ Ask yourself: 'How am I when I am at my best?' (This just puts you into a great state for doing this exploration!)
- ❤ Stand or sit in your 'true belief' spot and think of a belief you hold utterly and completely. It might be that the sun must rise tomorrow or that you

have to breathe to stay alive. If you are successful in your career, it might be a belief about your absolute ability to do what you do well.

- 💜 Pay attention to what is happening to you as you think of this belief.
- 💜 Tick off the qualities of your image against those on the list. Do this in your head or by writing them down.
- 💜 Do the same for the sounds you hear and the feelings you get.
- 💜 Notice where you look. How are you standing? What's your breathing like? Get the configuration as exact as you can. Stand in it for as long as you need to get a really, really strong sense of it.
- 💜 Now move to the 'want to believe' spot and think about something you want to believe but don't yet.
- 💜 Pay attention to what is happening to you as you think of this belief. Notice where you look. How are you standing? What's your breathing like? Get the configuration as exact as you can.
- 💜 Check off the qualities in the same way you did before.
- 💜 What's different between the qualities of the images, sounds and feelings of this belief and the true belief?

When you know the qualities of a 'true belief' you can change the qualities of a 'want to believe' belief to those of the true belief. You will be tricking your mind in a very clever way.

- 💜 Stand in the 'want to believe' spot, think of the belief you want to believe and play with the qualities until they are the same as those of the 'true belief'.
- 💜 Here are some of the things you may need to do:
  Step into it and see it through your eyes.
  Adjust the image's brightness or proximity to match the true belief.
  Change the tone or location of the sounds.
- 💜 When you notice yourself getting 'true belief' feelings associated with your new belief, you are on the way to building it into your system.
- 💜 Make a note of what happens. And if it isn't quite as you like it, make more changes until it is.

CONGRATULATE YOURSELF

The explorations you have been working through are ways of creating
empowering beliefs about yourself in exactly the same way that you
unconsciously created limiting beliefs as you grew up.

You've worked hard, so pat yourself on the back and say out loud, 'Well
done!' See your success for what it is and I know you'll continue to keep up the
good work because, in the words of Mark Twain:

There is nothing training cannot do. Nothing is above its reach. It can turn bad morals
to good; it can destroy bad principles and recreate good ones; it can lift men to
angelship.

BELIEVE IT!

The other frog continued to jump as hard as he could. Once again, the crowd of frogs
yelled at him to give up, he was going to die. He jumped even harder and finally made
it out. When he got out, the other frogs said, 'Did you not hear us?'

The frog explained to them that he was rather deaf. He had just assumed they were encouraging him to get out!

See how powerful beliefs are!

And now we're going to work on developing wonderful and empowering flirting states.

CHAPTER 6

DEVELOPING *fantastic flirting states*

We are the remnants of giant stars whose atmospheres were blown off in dramatic explosions and went on to form you and me . . . We are all, in the end, stardust.

Sara Russel and Conel Alexander

A romantic piece of prose? A myth from ancient lore? No! The quote comes from an article in the *New Scientist* on stardust and the origins of man. So we are all stardust – how wonderful. And we can all recapture and reactivate those stardust moments in our life.

LIFE – BITCH OR BEACH?

Some people think life is wonderful all the time. No matter what comes up they embrace it and enjoy it. Jeff Cain, remember him? He is a real sunshine person. People like Jeff know how to make themselves feel good, so good that no matter how painful things are they see the sunny side of life and feel great.

Feeling great – that's something we all need and desire. You know the feeling you get when everything is in harmony with you, when you feel at one with the world, when the outlook is positively rosy and you can taste and smell success in the air – *your* success? You have had those moments, haven't you, when you've been at your best, utterly and absolutely?

And perhaps you are thinking, 'Come on, Peta, life isn't like that.' It may not be at the moment and that's probably because you haven't been encouraged to experience that wonderful feeling of being yourself as often as you could have been. Believe me, you have had moments like this, even if it was a long time ago. Your unconscious remembers it, even if you don't. I bet there has been a moment, if only a fleeting one, when you've noticed that feeling of just being yourself with a smile on your face. It's the kind of instant when you feel so content you say things like 'This is me!' or 'This is how it should be.' You can have these feelings when you've been out walking on a beach or when you've been doing something you really enjoy or when you get the sense of a job really well done or when you've had a really rewarding, honest and meaningful conversation with someone. And the more you can feel like this, the more easily you are able to flirt with other people and spread the good-time feelings around, because you are overflowing with them yourself.

I'm not saying you have to be in an ultra-happy hyped-up state all the time, because you wouldn't be able to function. This is about being yourself and feeling as if you are in the right sliver of space for you. I'm asking you to think what it would be like to have these kind of feelings as a base state rather than moaning, complaining, feeling sorry for yourself, etc. They are the kind of feelings that allow you to think that no matter what happens, it's OK because you are OK.

When I feel good about myself, I feel most flirtatious and warm to others, and I am sure you do too. If you can develop more ways of feeling better more of the time, how much more likely are you to spread that to other people? A lot! You won't be able to help it!

So, in this chapter you will be travelling far into the realms of your mind on a search for all the wonderful moments you've experienced so that you can use them to create more 'life's a beach' moments.

YOU CAN PULL THE TRIGGER TO DELIGHT

Remember how in Chapter 4 we talked of how you can set a trigger to bring back an experience? It can be a word, or clicking your fingers, or perhaps making a fist. You may have noticed athletes making gestures before a race. These are their triggers to remember a great performance. Sports psychologists use these methods with the people they coach to keep them in 'peak performance state' and you can learn to keep yourself in 'peak flirting states' when you need to!

I use my fist as a trigger. I set the trigger by opening my hand, palm upwards, and imagining it could be a container of great experiences. When I get near the peak of the amazing experience I was recalling, I squeeze my fist. Now, in order to recall the experience, I squeeze my fist again.

Some people like to rub their forefinger and thumb together or click their fingers or pat their chest. One person I know decided they wanted to feel good when they turned on their computer, so they used the computer as a trigger and linked it to a great experience. Other people have a word that motivates them. A finger-click trigger has the double advantage of being physical and auditory.

FLIRTING STATES

I usually ask people in my flirting classes what they think would be a great state of mind to be in to flirt naturally and wonderfully. The most popular are feeling confident and playful.

What states of mind would put you in the mood for flirting? Pick a few. Here are some suggestions: confident, playful, curious, excited, anticipating, accepting, loving, sexy, fascinated . . .

MY IDEAL FLIRTY STATES

Write down five states that you think would really get you in the mood for flirting:

1

2

3

4

5

We're going to set a trigger for a particular state now and later you can create a cocktail of the states that really get you high for flirting!

SETTING YOUR TRIGGER

- ❤ Select a physical movement or a word or a scene as your trigger.
- ❤ You've had times or experiences, haven't you, when you were [choose a state]. Perhaps it is a time when you were at your best. Perhaps it was when you were a child. Take whatever comes up as you become aware of the experience. . .
- ❤ Make sure you are back in the experience when you remember it. See it though your own eyes.
- ❤ What are you seeing?
- ❤ What sounds are present?
- ❤ What feelings are you getting?
- ❤ Focus your attention on the place in your body where the feelings are strongest.
- ❤ Get your trigger ready.
- ❤ Imagine those feelings expanding out to your whole body and coming back in on themselves, like a wave.

- ❤ Keep doing it.
- ❤ Just as you are about to come to the peak of the experience (don't wait until you get there or it will be too late), make your gesture, say your word or see your scene. You are firing your trigger to coincide with the peak of your flirtatious state. Just as Pavlov conditioned his dogs to salivate (get into peak appetite state) when they heard the bell, so you can condition yourself to get into a great state when you fire your trigger.
- ❤ *Now think of what you did or didn't eat for dinner last night.*
- ❤ Wait a couple of minutes and fire your trigger again. What do you notice? Are you getting the experience back, even if vaguely? What feelings are you getting? Are they strong or mild?

If the experience doesn't come back so strongly when you fired the trigger, do the exploration until it does. You'll get it soon.

The reason I asked you to think of dinner was to get you out of the state you created and to allow you to test the trigger. Always make sure you do that before trying to fire it.

Congratulate yourself if you created your trigger and it worked. You just learned something very useful. If it didn't work, remember there's no failure, only results. You might not have got the result that you wanted. So what, just try again until you get the result that works for you. This is important because, like many of us, you have probably learned to associate failure with closure. So, banish the word 'failure' from your vocabulary and when you feel yourself about to say that you failed, learn to say instead: 'I didn't get the result I wanted *yet!*' This presupposes that you will get it sometime and you are encouraged to try again!

Remember that to become a SuccessFlirt, you need to participate in the process. The more you try things out, even if they seem a little strange, the more you will develop ways of really creating those fantastic flirty states. Like this, you can feel more resourceful and more hopeful more of the time and be more deliciously flirtatious.

LIVING IN PARADISE

I bet you know someone who always expects the worst. They generally get it. Funny, isn't it, how people who are positive and optimistic usually get what they expect too!

Wouldn't you like to be positive and optimistic more of the time? Right from the moment you wake up each day?

You've got to get up every morning with determination if you're going to go to bed with satisfaction.

George Lorimer

Do you want to feel good in the morning and focused on all the possibilities of a new day? Do you want to be able to start your day with sunshine even when there are clouds in the sky? This could well boost your ability to be nice to people and interact positively with them!

WAKE UP IN PARADISE

This exploration is simple. By asking yourself good questions, you will lead yourself to search for positive experiences. Think of the difference if someone asks what are you happy about as opposed to what annoys you!

You can ask yourself these questions any time you want and get all the answers you need to set yourself up for a great day in paradise. It's just a question of *what* you focus on. Is the glass half empty or half full? You choose!

Ask yourself these questions every morning.

Come up with two or three answers to these questions.

You can write them out if you want to.

Repeat your answers in your head with real meaning or out loud.

With each answer, work out what feelings arise, where they are, what they are like. Describe them to yourself and sense them fully.

If you find answering difficult, simply add the word 'could'. For example: 'What *could* I be most happy about in my life now?'

- What am I happy about in my life now?
- What am I excited about in my life now?
- What am I proud about in my life now?
- What am I grateful about in my life now?
- What am I enjoying most in my life right now?
- What am I committed to in my life right now?
- Who do I love? Who loves me?

(adapted from the work of Tony Robbins)

GO TO BED TO DREAMS OF PARADISE

Have you ever fallen into bed at night still running through the events of the day just ended? How do you think that affects how you dream and how you wake up?

Things happen to us all the time and some are positive and some not so positive. What often holds us back from feeling good and light enough to flirt is that we remember the not so positive stuff and run it through our minds. Sometimes this continues until we go to sleep and if you've ever found yourself waking up in the morning in a pretty lousy state, assuming you haven't got a hangover, it's probably because you are still wearing yesterday's emotions. You take off your dirty clothes and put them to wash, but how often do you wash off your soiled emotions? Sometimes a simple ritual can make all the difference between waking up looking forward to the next day and waking up feeling lousy.

And how much more flirtatious and disposed to be charming to other people are you likely to be when you wake up feeling happy and excited as opposed to miserable and still running through yesterday's rubbish? I don't think I have to tell you the answer to that one!

So, before you put your head on the pillow, wouldn't it be nice to wash away the day? I recommend that you take a shower each night and while you do so, take two minutes just to be quiet and imagine the shower washing all the day down the drain, leaving you fresh for tomorrow.

Another way, if you have a garden, is to find a spot that you like, stand there, barefoot if possible, and imagine all the woes and worries and stresses of the day just sinking down into the earth through your feet. Do this for a couple of minutes. If you live somewhere without outside access, just imagine them sinking below the floor through the next floor until they reach the earth.

This is a great way to let go of the day.

SETTING YOURSELF UP FOR TOMORROW

Every night before you go to sleep and dream, you have the opportunity to review your day, remember the good times and decide on how you will be tomorrow.

Ask yourself these questions every night:

- What great things happened today?
- What have I learned today?
- What questions do I want answered in my dreams?
- How do I want to be tomorrow?
- How can I use tomorrow to become more flirtatious?

As you lay your head upon the pillow you can just allow all those wonderful things to flow into your sleep and create new desires and dreams for your future. This is better than wishing on a star – it's specific, it focuses you and sets you up to move in the direction of your dreams.

What dreams do you have for your life, your relationships, your career and your well-being? Do you dream of flirting with life?

(adapted from the work of Tony Robbins)

THE GREATEST STATE OF ALL

I am sure you've had what I call droolingly desirable moments – the ones were you were so juiced up and ready to go for it that even thinking about it makes you blush. These are great states to be able to recall and they really add an edge to the kind of flirting that says: 'I want you!' We could call this state 'Beforeplay'! It's like mentally tickling yourself to turn on to the most wonderful feelings. Why not try it and see?

A DROOLINGLY DESIRABLE MOMENT

Think of a droolingly desirable moment in your life.

1   See what you saw, heard what you heard, smell what you smelt, taste what you tasted.
2   Turn up the brightness of the picture and double the size of it. Make it three-dimensional if it isn't already.
3   Turn up the volume and create surround-sound.
4   As you experience certain sensations in your body, notice where they start. Is it your head, toes, arms, heart, chest, stomach?
5   Enjoy the deliciously tasty glittering sense of that feeling.
6   Focus on where the feeling is strongest.
7   Breathe into the feeling . . . and just inhale and exhale a few times.
8   Keep breathing like this and imagine moving the feeling from where it starts to the base of your spine, then up your back to the top of your head. Imagine it travelling down your front through your heart and stomach to between your legs and back up again.
9   Run the feeling like a loop round your body until you feel even better!
10   When the feeling intensifies to near peak, set a trigger or add it to your other trigger!

DESIGNER STATES

What other feelings do you want to be able to recreate in the magic mixer of your mind? Would you like to be confident, open, excited, motivated, brave, carefree, at peace . . .? These wonderful states of being will all set you up for great flirting!

Write out what you want and we'll set it in motion and build a 'designer' state of mind that is ideal for flirting.

I am ....

MIX YOUR OWN GREAT-STATE COCKTAIL

So now you have the ingredients, it's time to start mixing. You are your own bartender, in charge of the cocktail creation. You can create feelings that you shake and spin around in your body, blending them into something delicious and new.

The idea is that you learn to mix cocktails of great states for different occasions. There may be times when you want to be excited and adventurous and others when you want to be calm and confident. You can choose!

- ♥ Decide on the three most delicious designer states you want to put in your cocktail.
- ♥ Repeat the previous exercise for all three states. Take a break – think of something mundane – between setting each state and between creating the last state and firing it off.
- ♥ Set the same trigger for each state.
- ♥ Notice how you feel when you fire it off.

Do this as often as you want to feel really good!

Not every method works for everyone. Some people find it easy to get into flirtatious states, like my neighbour David. He just turns on an imaginary switch and he's ready to go. Others need to relax or get a sense of strength and balance to be in the mood to feel good about themselves and be ready to flirt at the drop of a smile.

BREATHING INTO POWER

Have you ever had that feeling of being out of kilter or off balance? When you are like that, it's difficult to be strong and purposeful. Here's a great Aikido exercise that will automatically centre and align you. That would be a great way to be before a negotiation or a presentation or even going up to someone at a party and starting a conversation, wouldn't you say? Try it and see how it works for you.

GETTING STRONGLY CENTRED

Take some time and find a quiet place to do this exploration where you won't be disturbed. If you can get a friend to read it to you, great. If not, read through the guidelines first and then do it yourself – it's relatively easy.

- ❤ Think of something or someone that irritates or bothers you.
- ❤ Notice how thinking about this affects you. Notice the feelings it generates in your body and how you feel.
- ❤ Now think of something mundane, like how high the ceiling is.
- ❤ Stand with your feet about six inches apart.
- ❤ Locate a point about two inches below your navel. The name for this is 'hara' or 'one point'. It is considered to be your centre and is also the centre of your sexual energy. (You'll find out later how powerful this is.)
- ❤ Fix your eyes on something in front of you. (This is to stop your eyes from wandering and distracting you.)

THOSE INFERNAL VOICES

Some of the most common factors that prevent people from flirting wantonly and with lots of fun are the internal obstacles we construct for ourselves. You have the choice to be your own best motivational coach or the person who puts every conceivable barrier in your way. Are you a coach or a barrier builder? Before you can learn to flirt in a relaxed and natural manner, you may have to have a word with your barrier builder and turn it into a coach.

One of the ways we motivate others and ourselves is with words. How do you talk to yourself? Is it like Geoff?

GEOFF'S STORY:
A Quiet Night

Geoff's getting ready to go out. His friend Ed is sitting on the bed. As Geoff looks in the mirror he hears, 'God, you look terrible. Look at that hair, it's all lanky and greasy. And you've got a spot coming. Ugh, it's a big one and it's so red. Everyone will notice it. You're so skinny. Girls are supposed to like bums and you haven't got one and what's more, your teeth are crooked and your nose is too big. They'll see you coming a mile off . . . I don't know why you are even bothering. You'll only freeze when you see a girl you fancy. Remember the last time? You've just got no confidence . . .'

'Shut up, shut up, shut up! Go away!' Geoff said. But he wasn't talking to Ed, because Ed hadn't said a word. Geoff was talking to himself. . .

Ever done that? Of course you have, we all have. We can be our own worst enemies.

What if instead you were your own best friend? You wouldn't talk to yourself like that then, would you?

BEING YOUR BEST FRIEND

Who do you talk to most? Your friends, your family? Your colleagues? No! Your favourite conversation partner is yourself! Most of us have an amazing dialogue with ourselves and most of the time it's not pleasant! So, how much better would it be if you could learn to talk nicely to yourself? Remember that you have to flirt with yourself before you can flirt with anyone else!

FANTASY VOICES

- ♥ Start looking out for the times when you badmouth yourself to yourself. When you become aware of it, train yourself to say 'Shut up!' *in a very sexy voice.*
- ♥ Make a list of the bad things you say to yourself and how you say them.
- ♥ Look at your list and replace each item with some new words, words that you want to hear. Add what type of voice you want to hear saying them.
- ♥ For example, when Paul started telling himself, 'She won't fancy me' or 'She'll laugh at me', instead he wanted to hear 'Pounce on me, take me, hold me in your strong paws, you lion, you!' in a woman's voice which was 'quite strong and very heady'. He already knew that voice in his head.
- ♥ When Naomi heard her own fearful voice running scared whenever a man got interested in her she wanted to hear herself saying, 'Naomi, you are a beautiful sexual woman. You entice men. They can't help it – you are irresistible.'
- ♥ Stephen wanted to imagine a woman lying beneath him saying, 'Don't stop, yes please,' over and over again, faster and faster.
- ♥ Tom wanted to hear that voice of the radio announcer who commentated on the bike racing saying: 'And Tom Hancock has done it, he's won the title for the tenth time!' And he wanted to hear the sound of women's voices at a

REFRAMING THE PICTURE CHANGES ITS ASPECT

Some people constantly focus on the negative. But for every negative there is a reverse. Something that appears negative can be turned round to reveal its other, more positive side.

For each negative attribute, you can come up with several positive attributes to counterbalance it. Here's an example to give you an idea. Get creative with this stuff. It can be fun. It even makes a great party game!

- I'm too short.

- Some women love men the same height as them – their lips meet naturally (and the rest!)
- Nice things come in small packages.
- Tom Cruise is very short and he is a big sex symbol!

REFRAMING

- Reframe the phrases below. Be creative!
  I'm too old to meet a man.
  I'm too skinny.
  I've got a small penis.
  My breasts are too small.

I'm too aggressive.

I'm too overpowering.

- 💜 Then reframe the unhelpful things you say about yourself.
- 💜 And then we're done!

A FINAL (NICE) WORD. . .

Spend as much time as you can exploring how to set great triggers for great feelings. Use the 'Wake Up in Paradise' questions regularly and look out for things to reframe for the better. Soon this will become a way of life and no matter what happens you will be able to see some good in it.

In creating delicious flirtatious states for yourself, together with a sense of balance and calm, and a motivational voice in your ear, you set yourself up for much more positive interactions with others. Remember, the key to successful flirting is to start out feeling good so that you can transmit this to others.

And now you know what it is like to feel good, we're going to work on developing two key flirting aids: your voice and your body!

CHAPTER 7

VOICE AND *movement*

YOUR VOICE: A POWERFUL TOOL

Your voice is an instrument that can send waves of pleasure directly to another person's body.

Richard Bandler

The voice is a powerful instrument of communication. It can make or break your ability to affect people. Surveys conclude that over a third of meaning is conveyed in the tone of your voice.

Speaking is something we all do on a daily basis and no matter what it is that you want to convey or evoke, a great voice will enhance beyond measure your ability to communicate effectively.

This chapter is designed to make you aware of the value of a great voice. It offers some explorations that are designed to start you on the quest for your great voice. If you think your voice needs serious work, however, visit a speech therapist or a voice trainer.

DEVELOPING YOUR NATURAL VOICE

Have you noticed during a conversation that people may turn away, forget you, or even ignore you? That may be because your voice isn't representing you as best it can.

Once you find your natural voice, you may feel better, be more effective, and be listened to. The well-used voice has a 'feel-good' sound. It builds the speaker's confidence and makes a positive impression on others.

Dr Morton Cooper

What would it be like to use your voice to persuade, inspire, excite or seduce people into your life? Some people do it naturally. Sean Connery's voice exudes power, strength, confidence and oodles of sexuality. Some people have to work at it. Margaret Thatcher used to have a fairly high voice, but with expert help she lowered it and added tonal variety and depth. I think this had a major effect on her electability!

People often think that the voice they have is the one they were given and it can't be changed. Dr Morton Cooper, former Director of the Voice and Speech Clinic at UCLA Medical Center, estimates that over 50 per cent of us misuse our voices. If you have a weak or nasal voice, or if your voice sounds very breathy or squeaky, you may be misusing your voice. The great news is that *this can be changed*. It may be that you have just got into 'bad voice habits'. Dr Cooper believes that voice training is about bringing out the star qualities in your voice.

The voice is one of nature's most powerful flirting tools, because it just doesn't go into our ears, it hits our body with waves of wonderful or painful sounds. Voices create feelings in other people. Think of the possibilities.

Many of the participants in my flirting classes have benefited from developing their best voice.

CHRIS'S STORY:
'I Want to Sound Like a Lover, Not a Decorator!'

Chris's voice was *not* the kind of voice that sent sexually enticing messages to women. In fact, when he met new women, Chris always seemed to wind up doing their decorating!

Chris's voice was screechy and Lynne, a voice therapist, told me that his voice was too high for his height. She worked with Chris to lower his voice and got some amazing results. When Chris got used to talking in his new, lower voice, it created other subtle knock-on changes in him – his posture, for example, became more balanced and erect. Generally, the effect of knowing you sound good is to make you feel good. For Chris this was the confidence builder he needed to get started with being more flirtatious.

ALICE'S STORY:
'My Voice Is Too Quiet'

Alice was a teacher. She wanted to have a more assertive voice. When she was young her sick grandmother had lived with the family and Alice was always being told to be quiet. She learned how to do it so well that a quiet voice became the norm for her.

When Alice learned to access her more assertive voice, she found it so much easier to convey her message to the kids she taught.

HOW DID I GET THIS VOICE?

When you learned to talk you may have been affected by many influences:

- ❤ You will have imitated your nearest and dearest, your peers, your environment.
- ❤ You may have changed your voice as a form of antidote to the voices you disliked as a child – maybe your mother had a piercingly shrill tone and you adopted a quiet voice in defence. Perhaps your father had a 'wimpy' voice and you've created a barking tone as compensation.
- ❤ You may have changed your voice because of hurtful things people said to you about it.

- You may, like Alice, have learned to put a lid on your voice in order to keep other people happy.
- Maybe your voice got stuck in the wrong place at puberty, like Chris's.

MALE VOICES: *The Puberty Effect*

Constance Lamb, a voice trainer and actress, told me that because puberty is a time when most of us experience disturbing hormonal changes, guys' voices sometimes get stuck at too high a level as they struggle to maintain a balance in their changing tonalities. The good news is that it can be changed!

YOU CAN CHANGE YOUR VOICE

Your voice is not a tape recording you were stuck with at birth – it is an instrument you can learn to play well.

If your voice is frequently hoarse, too soft, too high or low, breathy or monotone, voice training may enable you to develop a more professional voice – and this is not just about sounding sexy and inviting, but also about being assertive and interesting.

Can you honestly say to yourself, 'I give great voice, baby'? Can you use your voice to make someone feel touched before you even touch them? How useful might this be in a flirtatious encounter or a negotiation, or even when you want to complain?

VOICEPLAY 1: WHAT'S YOUR VOICE LIKE NOW?

Before you begin to work on your voice it might be useful to check what it is like now. Make a 15-minute tape recording of your voice. Don't read aloud, just talk about something you love doing. Use this as a base line from which to improve and check back and notice the changes as you develop your best voice.

CHECKING YOUR PITCH AND TONE

Dr Milton Cooper has a great exercise for discovering your natural pitch level as well as your correct tone:

- Say 'Ummmm-hmmm' using rising inflection with the lips closed.
- If the sound you produce is in your right voice tone, you will feel a tingling or vibration round the nose and lips.
- If your voice pitch is unnaturally low, you will feel too much vibration in the lower throat.
- Keep saying the 'Ummmm-hmmm' until you feel that vibration in your lips.
- That is your natural voice coming out. Do this as often as you need to become aware of your natural voice.

Note: If you have already worked on your voice or are happy with the voice you have and it is not strained, obviously you can choose not to do the exercises. Some people think that the only good voices are low sultry ones. We all have different voice pitches but the key is to modulate and tone up our natural voice rather than trying to assume a false voice that strains us.

There are plenty of speech therapists and voice trainers who can help you if you need further training and Dr Cooper has produced several books, tapes and videos on the subject of the voice which are listed in the Resource section.

VOICEPLAY 2: FLEXING YOUR VOICE

We know that finding your right pitch and tone is important, but you may want to have different types of voice for different occasions. You will not want to use your public speaking voice to seduce a lover, although you may want to add a few seductive tones into your public speaking!

Did you know that you can modulate your natural voice according to which part of your body you are focusing on and breathing from when you speak?

'I'm Too Sexy'

Spencer has a wonderful voice that growls from deep down. It's a really sexy voice. The only problem was that Spencer used this voice in all situations!

Spencer tended to project his voice from below his navel, which was great for flirtatious encounters, but too soft for work presentations. He benefited from learning to bring his voice out from a different place.

WHERE DO YOU SPEAK FROM?

In this exploration you are going to discover what your voice sounds like when you speak from different parts of your body.

- ❤ Focus on your nose and imagine your voice that comes from there. Pinch your nose and say 'Hello' from there. Be aware of the tone.
- ❤ Now focus on your throat. Breathe into it and imagine your voice coming from there as you say 'Hello' again. Compare this voice to the voice from your nose.
- ❤ Next focus on your chest. Breathe into it, imagine your voice coming from there and say 'Hello'. This time the tones should sound deeper and more resonant. You may feel a vibration in your chest.
- ❤ Finally focus on a spot 2 inches below your navel (your hara point). Imagine you are speaking from down there and say a sexy 'Hello'. You should feel the vibrations and notice the difference.

Where should I speak from when?

- ❤ *From your nose:* This is not a place to speak from! It sounds whiny and unattractive. If you have a nasal pitch, I'd advise you to get some help – it can be rectified and you will notice how much more attractive you can sound.
- ❤ *From your throat:* This is great for drawing attention to yourself, screaming, warning someone of danger and expressing excitement.

💜 *From your chest:* This deeper voice has more resonance and is great for public speaking and commanding authority.

💜 *From your hara:* This is definitely a sexy voice. Speaking from down there will create a *frisson* in the person you talk to. It's great for whispering sexy nothings to your lover!

JUICY VOICES HAVE MORE FUN

There are some people whose voices just seem to ooze sexuality in their juicy rich tones. Wouldn't it be useful to be able to speak like this sometimes?

This exploration is designed to juice up your voice, so be sure to go for it!

WARMING UP YOUR VOICE

Find somewhere where you won't be disturbed to do this.

Think of a time when you had a really juicy moment in your life and say the following 'words' with as much meaning as possible:

💜 *'Oooooooooh!'* (Something juicy has just been presented to you.)

💜 *'Aaaaaaaah. . .'* (You are sighing with relief, as when getting into a warm bath after a long day.)

💜 *'Mmmmmm.'* (You are deeply excited by a new prospect.)

💜 *'Yes pleeeeeeaaaaaaaseeee!'* (You want something so badly you are begging for it!)

Now you can have some fun flexing your voice.

VOICEPLAY 3: BEING YOUR OWN VOICE COACH

If you don't have a serious voice challenge but just want to improve your voice you can become your own voice coach at home. You can 'model' the voices you admire.

There are three guidelines I advise you to follow here:

- model someone of the same sex
- model an adult voice
- model someone who conveys in their voice the qualities you want to convey

MODELLING A VOICE

In modern language courses now, they encourage the students not to speak *after* hearing the foreign language sentence but *while* they are listening to it. They have been using this technique at the University of California, San Diego, and it consistently produces results far superior to the traditional method.

This method will be very useful to you when working with your voice.

For this exploration, you will need to have access to a tape recorder.

- Make a 10-minute starting-point recording of your own voice. Don't read aloud, just talk. Talk about something you enjoy.
- Make a 10-minute or so tape of a voice you want to model. If you know someone who speaks on the radio and sounds great, then make a tape of that. You can make additional recordings during their performance, if it's a presentor, so that you have a longer tape. Perhaps it's someone on the TV, a newsreader or an actor. Make a video of them. Look at audio books. They are generally read by great actors with amazing voices. Check out if there is one that appeals to you and buy it.
- Listen to the tape of the voice you want to model all the way through. This way you will have a sense of the whole content.
- Choose a sentence that you want to work with. Listen to it a few times and begin to say it at the same time as the model voice.
- Rewind the tape and repeat it as many times as you feel necessary. Don't try too hard – relax and speak, relax and speak. Your brain can do it automatically, just like walking or breathing.

- ♥ Keep working with different sentences on the tape until you have completed them all.
- ♥ Now make another tape of your own voice and compare it with your original tape. When you are happy with the results, stop.

If you want to learn more voice variations, make a tape of another voice you admire and model that.

Now that you know you can tune your voice like a fine instrument, you can try out the different pitches and tones in interacting with people!

MOVE THAT BODY

Whatever the brain can organize, the body will execute.

Robert Masters

BODY = MIND = BODY

Heidi, a participant in my flirting class, said, 'This made me realize I spend too much time in my head and not enough time in my body.' How right she is. Flirting is not just something you think about in your head, it is a way of being.

It is now a common belief that the mind and body are not separate. They are part of one system. What goes on in the mind is held and acted out by the body. Conversely, we can affect our mind with our body.

Try this out to see how the two are linked:

- ♥ Look down, slump your shoulders, frown and then try to think about being really happy.
- ♥ Look up, sit up straight, open your body, breathe deeply and smile as you try to think about being depressed.

It isn't easy to have an emotion when your body is doing completely the opposite, is it? As your physiology is such a strong partner, it makes sense to work on your body and create an environment that fosters good feelings!

DANCE: A LIBERATING CONNECTION

Dancing is a wonderful way to free up your body. It can be done alone or done with others. It can be done to strict steps or it can be freeform. It is a great form of self-expression and a way of interacting with someone else . . . and deepening the connection. Just go to any salsa bar and watch the very ordinary-looking guys who are great dancers. You will see them sidling up to gorgeous women and moving with them. The women respond because dancing is sexy. The guys are enticing the women with their sensual movements!

Dancing can also be a powerful female flirting signal when used in the right way. I asked men in my workshops what spiritual, mental and physical qualities they looked for in a woman. Over 70 per cent of them said they liked women who were in touch with their bodies.

WHAT DOES DANCING MEAN TO YOU?

When you think of having to dance, what does that conjure up? One reason I include dance as the primary bodywork in my classes is that so many people don't dance because they think they can't do it properly. They have body memories of awkward attempts and when they get in a situation where they have to dance, they freeze.

You can build far better memories into your cells. A good way to start is by saying to yourself, 'I can learn to reactivate the dancer in me.' Then check out the Internet or a local newspaper or library and book yourself into a dancing class. There are plenty to choose from. I like merengue, because it's a sexy and easy-to-learn Latin American dance. You'll soon find out what is right for you.

I'll leave you with the words of Julia Gardner, dance teacher *extraordinaire*:

There is no 'right' when it comes to dancing – just be yourself and feel the rhythms and energies from within.

Move with your soul, not with your feet!

Think of dancing as having a great conversation with yourself, not just with other people!

MODELLING MOVEMENT: A NATURAL WAY TO LEARN

Modelling someone who moves well is a great way to learn. It's how children learn – but adults can do it too!

Imagine for a moment trying to walk and being conscious of every muscle and bone movement you have to make to take one tiny step . . . Confused? Of course! I bet you can't even take a step thinking like that. You didn't learn to walk like this – you learned by trying and by modelling.

PETA'S STORY:
A Swimmer Evolves

When I first started swimming for exercise, I had only the body memories of myself flapping a vague semblance of breast stroke with my aching neck holding my head out of the water.

I had noticed several swimmers who seemed to move gracefully so I started to follow one of them underwater. I imagined my arms and legs were linked to hers by a fine thread. I felt myself moving in synch with her as I modelled her movements. My whole swimming style changed.

I never did get to thank that wonderful swimmer, but I shall always remember how my body learnt so much from hers.

MODELLING MOVEMENT

So, what happens when you imagine you are a fabulous mover and your body is flowing in time to the music?

- First of all you need to have watched some good dancers or movers. Find some videotapes of people dancing, make your own videos, watch something on TV. Go to a club and observe quietly. Get some good reference memories of great moving or dancing.
- While standing, progressively relax your whole body from head to toe. Just focus on each part and say, 'Now I am relaxing my head, my shoulders, etc.'
- Remember how you are at your best and step into that.

- Watch a dancing videotape or imagine someone dancing or moving brilliantly. See them in front of you facing the same way as you are, so that you are watching their back.
- If you are imagining this, make the picture as bright as you need to really get the sense of it. Notice every detail of the movement. Add in any sounds that make the scene more realistic. Get a sense of the rhythm.
- Now imagine that person moving backwards towards you and melt into them. You will find yourself moving with them after a little practice.

Do this as often as you want to until it becomes second nature. Remember, repetition is the mother of all skills.

DANCING NATURALLY

If I could speak it, I wouldn't dance it.

Isadora Duncan

Dancing is a form of expression. For many people it is a very calming and energizing experience. To others it is a way of showing feelings that words cannot say. When you learn to express yourself in dance, you will open out your body to express intimacy or just enjoyment by dancing with another.

Learning to dance is not about being able to do it step by step. Good dancers move in whole form. Dancing is a fluid movement of mind and body.

All of us have a way of moving in the world and it tends to be the way we use most of the time. But when we can flex our body to move in different ways, we become more sensitive to the rhythm and flow of other people's movements. Great flirts are generally great movers!

When I think of perfect movement my thoughts always turn to animals.

SHIFTING INTO ANIMAL MOVEMENT

Have you noticed how naturally graceful some animals are? Even those that seem heavy and cumbersome have perfect ease of movement. I often wonder how it would be to have the grace and stealth and patience of my cat.

Animals have a lot to teach us about movement and energy and spirit and we can begin to learn some of their natural grace and poise too.

LISA'S STORY:
A Real Pussy Cat

Lisa wanted to move like her cat. She got off her chair and got onto all fours. She sat like a cat, walked around like a cat, arched her back like a cat and leapt around.

Afterwards Lisa said that she felt so peaceful when she was sitting and then as she leapt up she felt very alert and energized and the stretching exercise really lengthened out all her muscles and her back felt relaxed.

You may have picked a particular animal as a symbol of you at your best. If you want to use this animal for the next exploration, great. Maybe there is a particular animal that has great movement. Think about all the animals we usually associate with graceful movement, such as most of the cat family, gazelles, horses, birds. You don't have to assume all their moves – that might be a little difficult! – but pick something about that animal that sums up great movement to you.

FINDING YOUR ANIMAL

Whatever animal you pick, you can guarantee that by doing this exercise you will discover the ability to do new things and a much greater sense of flexibility in your head as well as your body!

- ❤ Think about which animal personifies the movements you would like to model.
- ❤ Make sure you have a good sense of how this animal moves. If you need to, watch some nature programmes on TV or go to the zoo.

Do this next part of the game only if you feel that writing it out first will help you. Some people feel better just imagining it.

- Write down the name of your animal.
- Visualize the animal moving. Find two or three movements that it does and become familiar with them.
- What is it about this animal that you feel drawn to?
- What is it about the way the animal moves that you admire?
- Describe two or three movements of the animal in detail.
- Now find a space where you can move around. You are just playing like a child, having fun and learning naturally.
- Find your space and sit or stand comfortably in the middle of it. Imagine your animal is in front of you with its back to you.
- Imagine stepping forwards and seeing, feeling and sensing the world as the animal does.
- Now begin to make the animal movements you have decided to model. If you need to get down on all fours, do so. Adopt whatever posture works best.
- Start to move like your animal. Really get into these movements! If you need to have some music playing, a simple two-beat rhythm will be fine. Make any sounds you need to make – and have some fun!
- When you are done, sit down and check your body from head to toe, gradually reassuming the posture of your best self!

So, how did that feel? Write your reactions down if you want. Be aware of what is happening to you. Awareness is a muscle that you can exercise all the time.

ELEMENTAL MOVEMENT

When you think of the elements – wind, water, fire and earth – what comes to mind? The elements are the basis of our existence and all of them exhibit very different qualities. They are also metaphors for different types of movement.

What qualities of movement are displayed by air, water, fire and earth? When I think of the wind, I think of a fluttering movement and also a fast whooshing movement. I think of waving my arms around in an 'airy fairy' way.

You'll get an opportunity in a moment to choose your own representations for each element. But first read how doing this exploration helped Graham to become more flexible.

GRAHAM'S STORY:
An Elephantine Task

Graham was a plodder. He moved slowly and put one foot methodically and determinedly in front of the other. His movements were heavy. He moved like the earth: solid, firm, deliberate. When he did this exploration he discovered new ways of moving which brought him a great sense of freedom. This came from being able to move from one way of holding himself into another. He found he was more able to approach people who were more energetic or more airy fairy than him by speeding up or slightly altering his natural way of moving. This is not about being false, it is about blending into someone else's world and making them feel more comfortable.

So, if you are wondering what on earth flexibility has to do with flirting, the answer is a lot. When you learn to move your body in different ways it has several benefits:

1   Loosening up your body loosens up your whole being so you become more relaxed and able to let go and flirt naturally.
2   You feel better about yourself because your body is learning to move gracefully or more powerfully.
3   You are better able to appreciate and get into another person's way of moving. This makes them feel you are like them and helps them become more open to you.

One of the things I've noticed about great flirts is that they are flexible and adaptable. If someone is flirting in a holistic way, you will always feel comfortable when standing next to them.

SHIFTING INTO THE ELEMENTS

Think of the positive and the negative qualities you associate with the different elements. For example, fire can be destructive or warming.

ELEMENT	QUALITIES
Fire	
Earth	
Air/Wind	
Water	

Now find yourself enough space to move around in, somewhere where you won't be disturbed.

Imagine you have a ball in front of you in the air. Pick an element and imagine both the ball and yourself having those elemental qualities.

❤ If the element is earth, the ball will be heavy, very solid and hard to move, like a cement block.

❤ If the element is air, the ball will be very light and easy to move, like a balloon.

❤ If the element is fire, the ball will be moving around fast. It will be almost weightless.

❤ If the element is water, the ball will flow and twist like a fish.

As you stand there, imagine you are the element earth, trying to move the ball. Remembering the movement qualities you assigned to earth, change your body movements to be more like that. If you have chosen 'solid and deliberate' as an earth-type movement, move like that. Push the ball around for a couple of minutes.

Do this for each element and notice the difference in your body after each one.

Take every opportunity to dance as freely, as often and as flexibly as you need to become a superb mover.

This will come in very useful when you learn how to gain deep energetic rapport with others.

Remember, as with all new things, practice is essential.

What we hope ever to do with ease, we must learn first to do with diligence.
Samuel Johnson

Now you've spent some time concentrating on two precious flirting instruments, your voice and your body, we are going deeper into your body on a journey into the realms of your sexuality. If you have picked up this book to learn social flirting, you may be surprised at how much you can benefit from this too.

CHAPTER 8

AWAKENING YOUR *sexuality*

Follow your bliss. Do what excites you, what makes you feel good.

Joseph Campbell

YOU ARE A SEXUAL BEING

It was the first day of the flirting class and Gary was about to start the merengue dance lesson. The room was quiet as Gary said: 'You are all sexual beings.'

A hush fell on the group, followed by giggles and a few blushes.

We *are* all deeply sexual beings and yet somehow we have learned to suppress our sexuality and sometimes feel embarrassed about it.

How much better might your attitude to your sexuality be if you had been taught how to really get in touch with it and enjoy it with passion and pride?

You may be reading this book because you'd like to become more flirtatious in your professional life. Perhaps you don't think a chapter on sexuality is for you. This chapter is not about using your sexuality to get what you want. It is about awakening and enjoying your sexuality to increase your well-being and natural flirtatiousness.

A good flirt feels good about themselves and is able to make others feel so good that they are drawn to them. When you have a great sex life (on your own or with a partner), you are more likely to feel good about yourself. I bet you've heard people suggest that someone who is always miserable and grumpy might be in need of good sex. This is probably true! Sexuality is part of your make up as a human being and if you enjoy a healthy sexuality, with yourself or with a partner, it is going to boost your ability to feel great about yourself.

This chapter is about how to expand your sexual awareness to harness your sexual energy in other areas of your life.

WHAT IS SEXUALITY?

Sexuality is not just about body friction and orgasms. Sexuality is an energy that runs through us, constantly driven by the inbuilt instinct to mate.

In this chapter I offer you ways to generate and enjoy this energy at will so you can harness it to make your life richer and more juicy! You can learn to love your body unashamedly, to experience bliss with or without a partner, and when the time comes to have a partner, to enjoy the experience fully. Does that sound exciting or does that sound exciting?

A TOUCH OF HISTORY

How touchy are you? Do you recoil when strangers touch you? Do you refrain from touching others? Do you feel guilty about touching yourself?

Sadly we have become less and less of a touching society. More men are closing down their natural touching instincts for fear of being accused of sexual harassment. More women hesitate to touch for fear it will be mistaken for a come on. Western people in particular are learning *not* to touch.

I believe that it is this withdrawal from touching and the isolation we experience in our society today that create many of the challenges we face in communicating with others. Touch is an essential and natural part of human communication. When you touch someone or are touched by them you are literally transmitting or receiving energy. You can touch another person in many ways – with simple friendly energy, with loving energy and with sensual energy. Great flirts know how to touch appropriately and effectively.

Thousands of years ago, in cultures where non-violence was a norm, children received constant touches, caresses and massages from the women in their tribe. Children were encouraged to explore their bodies and touch themselves. It is a natural way of gaining more awareness of your own body.

Today the Board of Education in one US state sacked a woman because she advocated promoting masturbation as an alternative to young teenage sex and unwanted pregnancies. In my humble opinion, it is a sad, sad world when people are condemned for promoting the most natural and pleasurable of activities.

What would it be like to regain an element of your childlike shamelessness and be able to experience the natural joy and that arises from touching yourself and others?

SELF-ABUSE OR SELF-LOVE?

Have you learnt to feel good about touching yourself in a sensual way that generates great pleasure?

Did any of the people who were in charge of guiding your life as a child and growing teenager ever say anything remotely encouraging to you about masturbation? If so, you are very lucky and you probably feel extra specially good about yourself. If not, take heart, you'll have an opportunity to feel good as you go through these pages.

Remember that flirting is about flirting first with yourself and then transmitting those feelings to others. If you want to flirt on a sexual level, you have to flirt sexually with yourself too!

SHONAGH'S STORY:
Self-Abuse

Shonagh was a 36-year-old accountant. She told me that without a man in her life she felt less alive and unwanted. She said she had forgotten how it felt to be sexy. She had not had sex with anyone for five years and by her own admission she thought it was over-rated. Shonagh thought that masturbation was something people resorted to when they were desperate. When she was five, her mother had caught her touching herself and she had slapped her while shouting that the Devil would get her if she continued to carry out his work.

How sad that someone should have been depriving herself all these years of the joy of self-love. Shonagh, like many people, was a victim of her mother's own learned shame. She was out of touch with her natural desires.

Are you in touch with your desires or are you depriving yourself of one of life's natural God-given pleasures? When people can't love themselves sexually they are missing out on a big part of life's natural pleasures and their glow can begin to fade. If this happens to you, it's unlikely you will be sending out healthy sexual signals!

This is avoidable when you learn to change your concept of self-abuse to self-pleasuring.

SUE'S STORY: *Self-Love*

Sue was single and happy. She knew that the right man would come into her life when she was ready. Meanwhile she wanted to keep sensing that juicy feeling of anticipation and explore her sexuality to the full. When she was 12 her cousin had given her an article on masturbation and the joys of multiple orgasms. What Sue read in that article led her to experiment and discover wonderful things about her body. Unlike Shonagh, no one chastised Sue for being curious and exploring her body!

Sue loved to pleasure herself. She would think about it during the day and then when she got home she would run herself a bath, light some candles and put on her favourite music. She loved to lie in the bath, glass of wine in hand, reading a piece of erotica from a novel that really turned her on. Sue reckoned that fantasies were great because with them you could explore all the sexual sides of yourself and know what you really wanted to do and what you would be happy to just fantasize about. She learnt a lot about her own body and experimented with different ways of giving herself pleasure.

Sue had been fed some wonderfully enabling and empowering ideas as a child. Her self-exploration will enhance her ability to really enjoy being with the lover she is destined to meet.

Who do you identify with more strongly, Shonagh or Sue? Do you indulge in quick and furtive episodes of masturbation and feel guilty or dissatisfied that you have to 'resort to' that, or do you luxuriate in the pleasure you can create for yourself?

In order for someone to really love you, you must first really love yourself.

That's one of those common-sense statements that have been around for years and how true it is. Here's another:

Self-love is not a second-class activity, it has an excitement and fun all of its own.

LEARNING TO LOVE YOURSELF AT YOUR BEST

Throughout this book I have emphasized how important it is to feel good about yourself. And sex is nature's own good-time drug! You can learn to enjoy your vibrant sexuality and feel good about it even if you don't have a sexual partner yet!

Before we begin to work on that it might be useful to know where you are now. The following exploration will allow you to explore your current attitudes and beliefs about self love.

Doing this exploration will arouse in you certain sensations. This is part of the process. Just be aware of them. The more you get to know your own signals and get in touch with your body, the more you will be able to develop your own ability to override things that are not useful, shift into the right gear and ease gently down on the throttle as you begin to generate ecstasy inside and out. By doing this exploration, you are opening up to the truth about yourself and this will enable you to move forward.

If during this exploration you discover beliefs that don't serve you, you can change them. You know how because we've worked on that already. And if you find yourself talking to yourself in the wrong way, you know how to create a voice that says what you really want to hear.

Before you begin you can say to yourself:

I am eager and curious to discover myself and whatever information comes up will be useful for my learning. I am ready to try something new.

ENTERING THE AROUSAL ZONE

Find a quiet place to work undisturbed and allow yourself plenty of time. Have something to write or draw with and some paper.

As you do the exploration, you will be talking to yourself, making images and getting body sensations. You will become more aware of what is going on in your body. If you need to stop to take note of how you feel at any time, do so.

Answer the following questions:

- 'Masturbation is . . .' Answer this quickly!
- What were the stories you heard about masturbation as a child? What did your parents say? What did your friends say?
- Do you masturbate?
- When you thought about that question what happened? Write down what images, sounds, thoughts came to mind. What happened in your body?
- If you do masturbate, how do you feel about yourself and the experience?
- Do you ever talk about masturbation?
- If you don't, what does the thought of discussing it do to you? Check the feelings in your body.
- If you don't masturbate, do you want to? If so, why, if not, what stops you?
- When you masturbate do you just do it hurriedly and forget about it or do you relish every moment?
- Have you ever experienced what you might term 'sexual bliss', with yourself or others?
- Do you ever explore different ways of self-pleasuring?
- If you have fantasies, how do you feel about them?
- Have you ever spent more than half an hour masturbating?
- Can you have an orgasm?
- Have you ever had multiple orgasms? (Men too.)

- ❤ If you haven't had multiple orgasms, would you like to?
- ❤ Have you ever used magazines, videos or tapes to masturbate to?
- ❤ How do you feel about using these props?
- ❤ Are there things you want to explore but feel uncomfortable about? If so, what are they?
- ❤ How would you like to feel about them?

Having explored where you are now, what wonderful things can you do for yourself even if you don't have a lover? Think about this and let the answers come up. Write them down if you wish to.

Congratulations on taking another step towards opening out to yourself.

What interesting information did you glean about yourself?

What do you want to feel about your sexuality?

Think about how you feel when you are really enjoying yourself and let go of any guilt.

Self-love is a wonderful and joyous experience and people who try to make you think it is taboo are interfering with your natural desires. It is also a great way to keep the works oiled in anticipation of what is to come. The more you explore your own sexuality, the more you will be able to freely enjoy great sex with a partner.

And self-love in the way I am prescribing here is actually a great way of flirting with yourself. Self-love, be it sexual or non-sexual, is the basis of being a great flirt and so what if you do start to attract lots of people to you? Even if you aren't in the market, it's just an added bonus. I'm not just talking about sending out sexual signals here, I'm talking about the kind of aura you give off when you are being like this. It's a sort of *je ne sais quoi* that attracts other people to you. The more you love yourself sexually, the more you will come across as a sexually attractive person.

From now on, I have chosen to refer to masturbation as 'self-love'. This is deliberate. It is designed to get you to think of it as something different. You can choose your own name, but make sure it is enticing!

THE PRINCIPLES OF ENERGY

One of the basic ingredients of achieving sexual bliss is to be aware of how your energy expands and contracts. Have you ever been around people whose presence just seems to fill a room? It's as if they have expanded some of themselves into the room. What about those people who seem to fade away into the background? It's as if they are trying to contract into themselves . . . It is useful to be able to both expand and contain your energy. When you want to have magical encounters with others, you will do so more readily if you learn to expand your energy outwards.

Sometimes we talk about people being vibrant. 'Vibrant' comes from the verb 'to vibrate'. Vibrant people literally send out energy vibrations. You can become a vibrant person *and* you can learn to vibrate as much or as little sexual energy as is appropriate. When you do this, people around you will sense something about you and those you want to will sense your sexuality too.

This is *not* about giving someone a sexual come on to get what you want. It is about accessing and giving out your natural deep-seated glow.

PERSONAL SPACE

If you think you haven't experienced different energy vibrations from people, think again.

When someone gets too close to you in a crowded train or at a social event, you may have experienced that shrinking feeling. And yet when someone you like gets close it's very different. A book on body language might tell you in feet or metres how much personal space people require. I don't work like that. Each culture is different and within each culture individuals vary in how close is close enough for them. You unconsciously know the boundaries of your own personal space because you react when someone comes too close. The more comfortable you are with people, the closer you let them get.

You are not just a sexual being, you are an electrical being. We burn energy and give it off. This is a scientific fact. Energy fields have been photo-captured in scientific experiments, appearing as a sort of halo around the body. Infra-red heat seekers which can detect human energy through solid mass are now standard equipment on many police helicopters.

Your personal space is the space you need to contain your own field of energy. It can expand or contract depending on your reactions to situations and other people. Think of the boundaries of your own personal space as a flexible resting state for your field of energy.

Some of the exercises that follow are designed to get you in touch with your own energy so that you can begin to sense other people's energy. When you can do that and can use your abilities to notice signals people are giving off, you will find it much easier to naturally adapt how close you get to someone according to what you sense about their personal space and levels of comfort.

You can feel your own energy. Try it for yourself.

SENSING YOUR ENERGY

- 💜 Rub your hands together very briskly for a minute, making sure you include your fingers and thumbs. Notice how that feels.
- 💜 Keep rubbing them together then let them separate a little and feel the space between your hands. You can imagine there is a ball in between your hands (there is – a ball of energy!) and try bouncing it. Whatever you feel, you are sensing the energy you generate.

USING YOUR ENERGY

You know we talk of people 'really making their presence felt'. Notice the language. It is full of clues to what really happens. We *do* feel the physical energy of other people.

The following exploration will help you to expand your energy and make your presence felt more – rather useful for a great flirting encounter, don't you agree?

MAKING YOURSELF FELT

♥ Stand in the centre of a room and take a minute or two to regulate your breathing and relax your arms and body.

♥ As you breathe in, imagine you are expanding your energy to fill the room. Imagine that it gets denser, thicker, as it expands and that it can go out to include the whole street, the town, the country, and so on.

♥ Relax and breathe. Now imagine you are a tiny speck in relation to the rest of the world. Notice how this makes you feel.

Practise this exploration as often as possible. It will increase your ability to make yourself felt.

EXPANDING AND CONTRACTING YOUR ENERGY

Sometimes we contract or expand our energy according to our reactions to others. People who have the knack of communicating successfully with others do this all the time.

Shrinking in Fear

Have you ever noticed how when you are in an unpleasant or challenging situation, maybe when someone is being nasty to you or you are nervous about chatting to someone new, you find your body stiffening and tensing? You may bring your arms and legs closer to your body or hold your breath. Your shoulders may hunch and you may bend forwards. It's almost as if you are trying to shrink into yourself and make yourself small.

You are contracting your energy.

People who are scared to flirt often overcontract and tighten in 'threatening' social situations. I have heard people describe this state as 'freezing up', 'feeling stuck' or 'being rooted to the spot'.

The following exploration is about becoming aware of what happens to your body in difficult situations. Then you can begin to relax and let go!

EXPERIENCE HOW YOU CONTRACT

- 💜 Think of someone you don't like or are a little intimidated by, perhaps a work colleague or a social acquaintance, even someone on TV.
- 💜 As you think about this person, check your body all over. What is happening? Are there areas of tightness? Be aware of them.
- 💜 Continue to think of the person and as you do, start to smile and breathe deeply.
- 💜 As you begin to relax, say to yourself something like: 'I can object to this person without screwing up my body.'

You may have met people who felt overwhelming. We even say we were 'bowled over' by someone. Interesting how our language is directly linked to what it is trying to describe. Some people are so overwhelming they put people off.

When meeting such people you might be tempted to contract your energy as a defence mechanism. But this can make you frozen or stuck, and, like this, you limit your ability to react and change the situation.

Contracting yourself too much is definitely not useful if you are about to chat someone up or enter a room full of people. You do want people to be aware of you, don't you?

Expansive Possibilities

Expanding your energy increases the range of your sensory perception and also your presence. You can send out more electrical charges – positive vibes that attract people to you. These vibes can be controlled by your focus and your breathing.

In my flirting classes, we sometimes play a game of 'sensing the energy'. Two people work together. One stands still with their eyes closed and the other person removes their shoes and approaches them. The object is to find out at what stage the person standing still can feel (not hear or see) the other person. They do this exercise once without doing anything out of the ordinary. What generally happens is that the person being approached doesn't feel the presence of the explorer until they are within a foot or two of them. Some people have to be tapped on the shoulder before they notice it. They then repeat the exercise while the person being approached literally imagines their energy expanding behind and around them. With a little practice it is possible to become quite accurate at feeling the person behind or around them from greater distances.

What might this have to do with flirting? Good flirts are very aware of what goes on around them and sensitive to the changes in other people. Often these changes are something that sensitive people can feel. If you can learn to feel people close to you, you are sharpening up your senses.

Next time you are walking down the street or standing somewhere, imagine your energy expanding out and try to feel the people behind you. The more you do this, the more sensitive you become to feeling energy. Try it out for yourself. It can be a great party game!

It's also a way of dealing with difficult people. . .

ENERGIZING DISCOMFORT TO COMFORT

- ❤ Think again of the person who makes you feel uncomfortable.
- ❤ Focus your mind on your hara point, 2 inches below your navel.
- ❤ As you breathe in, imagine you are drawing in the strength of the earth through your feet and the light of the sun through the top of your head.
- ❤ Now as you breathe in and out, smile (even if you have to force yourself) and gently imagine expanding your energy to cover the person you used to think intimidated you.
- ❤ What difference do you notice?

Next time you find yourself in a social situation, practise smiling and expanding your energy. If you are in a crowded area, imagine expanding it first to include those around you, then the entire street, then the world.

You may notice that when you expand your energy you can walk down a street and people will unconsciously move out of your way!

This is also a great technique for dealing with overwhelming people. When you meet them, instead of contracting your energy, expand it back out. They will sense you, just as animals sense a worthy opponent, and back off!

By exploring your energy and taking control of its movement, you are preparing for the next step – working with your sexual energy. Great flirts are often unconsciously moving their sexual energy around their body and outwards. This is why they seem to give off that special something that makes them desirable.

GENERATING SEXUAL ENERGY

Your sexual energy is the life force of your primal drive to mate. But you can harness this energy for many other things as well as giving off that sexually tinted glow that draws others to you magnetically!

Some people believe that the only way to perpetrate sexual arousal is by friction and that the end goal should be orgasm. People who have studied Eastern religions and philosophies have discovered that the sexual energy can be aroused without direct need for orgasm and it can be kept simmering and harnessed in many other ways. You can learn to have more input into how and when it is generated, and for what purpose.

THE BREATH OF SEXUAL ECSTASY

You can generate sexual energy with a combination of breathing and creative thinking.

SEXUAL ENERGY BREATHING

This exploration will help you to get in touch with the centre of your sexual energy and is a prelude to the next exercise, the juicy one!

- Stand with your feet about 6 inches apart.
- Breathe slowly in and out.
- Put your hands on your hip bones, fingers to the front, and feel the bowl-like shape of your pelvis.
- As you breathe in, sense your pelvis tipping forwards.
- Focus on this area and as you breathe in, imagine your pelvis is scooping up the energy.
- As you exhale, the pubic bone lifts forward and empties this energy into you.

Do this often – it relaxes you and will prepare you to expand your sexual energy.

Dr Peter Staats of Johns Hopkins Medical Institution asked 40 college students to plunge a hand into ice water and keep it there as long as they could stand it. Some students were asked to think of a preferred sexual fantasy as they did so. These students were able to endure twice as long as those who had neutral thoughts. They also experienced less anxiety!

Think how useful it would be to harness sexual energy whenever you felt nervous or concerned. And by the way, no one would know what you were thinking about, they would just sense you had a more powerful energy!

Now you are going to be moving away from pain towards long-lasting pleasure as you indulge in a little focused erotic fantasy!

UNLEASHING SEXUAL ENERGY

In this exploration you are going to learn to generate sexual energy and use breathing to direct it round your body, amp it up and turn it down. This is a simple exploration. Once you become familiar with it, you will want to do more of it!

Do this exploration when you are alone and have plenty of time to indulge yourself. You can do it sitting or lying down.

Read the instructions through as often as you need to get a sense of how to do it.

♥ Make yourself comfortable and relax.

♥ Breathe in and out slowly, focusing on the rhythm or sound of your breath, and slowly relax your body by moving your attention to each part, from head to toe, deliberately letting the individual muscles relax as you do so.

♥ Begin to focus on the hara point, about 2 inches below your navel, and breathe into it.

♥ As you breathe, gently begin to recall a very erotic or arousing sexual experience. It might be a fantasy or it might be a memory, but it is really exciting, something that really turns you on as you continue to breathe . . . and. . .

♥ Check your feelings. Are they strong enough? If not, adjust your images and sounds for optimum pleasure. Check your feelings again.

♥ Breathe in the experience, imagine it happening in your body right now and just let your body go into it.

♥ Completely surrender to the experience, but refrain from touching yourself yet.

♥ If you want to increase the flow of sexual energy round your body, you can move your hips, rock back and forth, open and close your thighs rhythmically or just move in any way that enhances the sensations.

♥ Now imagine looping these feelings from your sexual centre up your spine into your neck, over the top of your head and down through your throat, heart and solar plexus to between your legs and back up again. Do at least 10 loops.

- Let the feelings subside, relax and then generate them again. Loop them again. Keep doing this for as long as you are enjoying it.
- If you feel a desire to reach orgasm, try waiting an hour after you have let the feelings subside. The longer you can keep this going, the more you are learning to be in charge of your sexual energy.

What were your reactions to doing this? Did it feel good? What did you learn about yourself? You might like to make a note of your discoveries in your journal.

KEEP THE PILOT LIGHT BURNING

We are mostly taught that sexual arousal must be followed by orgasm. Generally when we experience sexual arousal at times that might be inappropriate to follow it through, we respond by contracting our energy and repressing the desire. It is the repression that leads to frustration. But you can learn to get mildly 'turned on' and turn it into a sensually motivating force which can be used in many situations!

When I first described this to one friend, she said, 'How can you be like that for hours and not *do* anything? It must be so frustrating!' The difference here is that you are giving those feelings expression and allowing them to bubble up and simmer down, which is very different from suppressing them.

Think of your sexual energy as the pilot light in your boiler. It's a real fiddle to relight it if it goes out. When it just burns there with a flickering flame, it is ready to spring into roaring action. The pilot light exists to save you the trouble of relighting the boiler each time you want heating or hot water. When you turn on the tap, it heats up instantly!

PRACTISE YOUR WAY TO ECSTASY

When you continue to do this on a regular basis you will find yourself becoming more easily aroused and able to generate sexual energy to create a variety of feelings, from just feeling nice and juicy to passionate desire. Then you can choose whether you want to send out a strong sexual vibration or a mild one!

If you are a man, you can arouse yourself to just before you get an erection and begin to precisely calibrate it so that it's just enough to generate some of that powerful testosterone but not enough to be obvious . . . if you know what I mean.

If you are a woman, you can just continue to do it and do it wherever you are, as long as it makes you feel good! Shopping in the supermarket, cleaning the car, ironing and working on a report can take on whole new meanings!

CONTINUING TO ENJOY THE EXPERIENCE

When you have practised this on your own at home and have gained the necessary delicate control of taking yourself to a gentle state of excitement without getting full blown, you may find it is something you can generate in other situations. Men may have to practise a little longer to find that 'just before it gets embarrassing' point whereas women can do it anywhere without drawing undue attention to themselves. All that people will notice is that you have a little bit more of a shine in your eyes and a flush on your cheeks and that you are glowing more!

- Imagine you have a pilot light in your hara point and think sexy.
- As you become mildly aroused, notice where the feelings are strongest.
- Breathe into that place and as you inhale, imagine the pilot light expanding into full flame and sending the resultant energy to all of your body, filling you with joy and smiles.
- As you exhale, imagine turning the pilot light down as the feelings subside until a small flame of energy remains flickering.

When you practise this regularly, you can experience exquisite moments and even mild orgasmic feelings from time to time.

Now that you are aware that you can unleash this sexual energy, we are going to explore how to prolong the pleasure when you really want to be sexual, first with yourself and then others.

A RITUAL OF SELF-LOVE

The function of ritual, as I understand it, is to give form to the human life, not in the way of a mere surface arrangement, but in depth.

Joseph Campbell

Self-love can be a furtive quick act or it can be a ritual of self-indulgence, fun and passion. Use your imagination for your self-love ritual and be creative. Anything goes!

Start thinking about your ritual a couple of days beforehand or as long as you can enjoy the anticipation. Do the sexual energy breathing progressively as the time approaches. Take your time, relax and make sure you have everything you need to make this a pleasure-dome experience. And remember the goal is not orgasm, but prolonged pleasure and ecstasy.

You might like to try out some of these suggestions:

- Get comfortable and begin to breathe using the sexual breathing exploration.
- If there are parts of your body that you have not caressed or explored, do so.
- Try a ritual touching exploration of your body from top to toe. Do it slowly, lingering over every uncharted part.
- Experiment with how you touch yourself. Slow down, speed up, move with a different rhythm.
- Allow erotic thoughts to come in and as you get into an erotic sexual fantasy, try bringing in the feeling of you at your best.
- Think of some wonderful ways you want your life to be and practise blending the life fantasies with the sexual fantasies.
- When you reach the point before the point of no return, stop! Let the excitement simmer down gently and wait a few minutes before you reactivate it.

FLIRT COACH

You can keep this going as long as you have time. When you finish, stay where you are for a while, continue to breathe evenly and rhythmically, recall the events in slow motion and keep breathing into them.

It is better to wear out than rust out.
Richard Cumberland

A ritual like this is wonderful because not only do you feel brilliant, but you are accepting and indulging your natural desires. You are learning to experience sexual sensations at will and enjoy the experience of sexual arousal as a way of being instead of something to be satisfied.

You can harness this energy to motivate you to do other things . . . and you can resonate this energy to others.

EXTREMES OF SEXUAL ENERGY

Your body can generate sexual energy at will or unconsciously. Imagine that your body is a boiler with a thermostatic meter and a pilot light. The meter measures sexual energy on a scale of 0 to 5: 0 is turned off, 1 is just bubbling under and 5 is all fired up and ready for hot sex!

When the pilot light is lit and on level 1, the process of turning the heat up or down is a simple one. When the pilot light is out on level 0, it is a much more difficult process to get the heat going.

Your body will respond to internal and external triggers by adjusting its level of sexual energy output. This doesn't mean it's a perfect system. In the same way that outside influences have buried our natural ability to flirt, we may have been subject to thoughts or situations that have disrupted the body's ability to generate appropriate levels of sexual energy. It doesn't matter how this happened, what does matter is that it is possible to change it once you recognize the pattern and to use the tools from this book to be more yourself.

IS YOUR SEXUAL ENERGY OUT OF CONTROL?

When you have smooth flowing, adjustable sexual energy you will become a very polished flirt. You will be giving out just the right amount of sexual energy for the situation and you will be in control of it and eventually, with practice, it will just happen automatically and appropriately.

Some people give off too much sexual energy too often and inappropriately, others don't give off enough sexual energy. Some have turned it off altogether! Whenever this happens, the sexual energy becomes unbalanced and so does the interaction between men and women.

THE 'NICE GUY' NO SEX SYNDROME

Johan was a great-looking 35-year-old professional guy. He was bubbly and appeared confident, but he just couldn't get his relationships with women to go from best friend to bed friend! He told me that he felt he'd lost touch with his sexuality. Johan, like many of the men I coach, suffered from 'nice guy' syndrome!

By 'nice guy' I mean men who are trying too hard to be non-threatening, accommodating and subservient to women by denying their natural selves. In his eagerness to turn down the sexual vibes Johan had turned off his pilot light. When he learned that it was OK to relight his sexuality, he became bed friends with his best friend!

When Lewis was 17 his girlfriend had asked him if he wanted to 'pounce on her'. As a healthy lad, of course he wanted to! But he thought she was testing him to see whether he was just after sex, so he said, 'No, I can wait.' She dumped him. Later his friend went on a date with her and called Lewis the next day to say, 'She's crazy.' Lewis had played the 'nice guy' and this highly sexed girl had lost interest! He learned that sometimes women want sex in the same way that men do and that it doesn't always pay to turn off when you are turned on!

WHAT MAKES A MAN SEXUALLY ATTRACTIVE?

I asked a group of women about the magic ingredients that make a man instantly attractive. For me, it is something they give off, an earthiness, a sense of confidence and of course the eyes and the smile. . .

Lesley said it was something she could see and smell: 'Some men just have an air of confidence, of strength, and it doesn't matter what they look like – they either have it or they don't.'

Then Karen jumped in and said, 'Do you know that feeling when you walk into a room and suddenly you come up against a wall of testosterone?'

Testosterone is the hormone that fuels the male sexual system. When a man has his sexual energy turned on, he generates more testosterone. Men who are very comfortable with and in touch with their own sexuality will generate more testosterone than those who are suppressing it. Karen wasn't far wrong when she said she could feel the 'wall of testosterone'. The testosterone causes the emission of particles called pheromones which women can sense. If you turn off the sexual energy, the person you are out to attract literally can't smell you and without that smell they don't feel any attraction!

At the other extreme, when people give off too much sexual energy too often, they create problems and confusion.

BAD GUYS

Why do you think women fall for bad guys? Bad guys generally don't have enough respect or thought for women to keep their energy at an appropriate level. Their pilot light *never* goes out but they are always burning on level 4.5! Women pick up on the sexual energy and if it is attractive enough to them, the personality flaws may well seem less important. Sexual magnetism is a powerful drug and we are primed to react to it automatically. My advice to girls who go for bad guys is to take a moment very quickly to look beyond the sexual magnetism before you get hooked!

GIRLS WHO GIVE OUT TOO MUCH

Women who don't like themselves very much or feel insecure often use the power of sexual magnetism to get what they want or to feel good because they know men are drawn to it.

There are practical reasons why women should learn to lower and raise their sexual output in the right way at the right time. Do you remember Rachel, who was running on top-level energy all the time? She learned that when she transmitted her sexual energy like that, she often got more than she bargained for. It can be dangerous!

What about Leanne, who just couldn't flirt with anyone she fancied? She was putting out sexual energy, but it was misdirected. That can get you into big trouble too. Leanne married the wrong guy!

WHAT DO MEN FIND ATTRACTIVE IN A WOMAN?

I was a guest on a TV show about sex appeal. The men in the audience were shown identical twins. One twin was dressed in short skirt, low-cut top, high heels and red lipstick. The other was wearing a velvet suit, had her hair up and wore pearls. The guys had to vote on which twin had the most sex appeal. Most of the men voted for the short-skirted twin. (Incidentally the only man who voted for the twin in the pearls was Robert Merril, the diet Pepsi model. He said the classy look turned him on!)

The great majority of men will always be attracted to a woman's overt sexuality. They are programmed for it, it's part of their genetic heritage. However, men do look for other things too.

When I asked a group of well-balanced, confident, sexy men what they wanted in a woman, their answers were pleasantly surprising. Aaron said he didn't have a type, but she had to be honest, caring and open to her own sexuality. Paul said he liked women who were in touch with their bodies and knew what they wanted. Denis said he liked a woman to be comfortable enough with her own sexuality to make the first move. Michael said he liked that quote about a woman being a chef in the kitchen and a whore in the bedroom!

Women don't have to be always firing on all sexual cylinders to attract a man, but they do need to feel comfortable with firing on all cylinders when they want a man to be attracted to them in that way! Giving out a little sexual vibe can be more initially attractive than a full-on 'come and get me' and then, when it gets to the stage where full-on 'come and get me' is appropriate, you can turn up that meter to 5 and go for it!

On the other hand women can learn to turn down their sexual meter to a much lower level when they don't want to be pursued.

Sex is a wonderful and exciting part of our natural life. We should always respect the presence of our sexuality in any encounter and moderate it accordingly. When you are flirting for sex, turn up that meter to no. 5. When you are flirting to attract someone but don't want sex straightaway, turn it up a little bit, say to no. 3, and when you are flirting professionally to make someone feel good, turn it to no. 1.5, which is just enough to add that edge to your encounter without being overtly sexual. We are all primed to respond to sexual signals and the strength of our response will depend on the strength of the signal.

BREATHING YOUR SEXUAL METER UP AND DOWN

Practise the sexual breathing exercises and get comfortable with your levels of sexuality. You know what it's like when you are fully sexually charged. By moving your sexual energy from where it starts through your back and round your body you can dissipate it, and by focusing on where your sexual energy starts and indulging in whatever turns you on, you can increase it. Play around with it – get fully turned on and then let it go. Soon you will become a naturally sexually charged person giving out just the right amount for the situation.

Four juicy rules for keeping your sexual energy in balance:

1   Always keep that sexual energy bubbling and the pilot light lit.
2   Turn it up to add that almost imperceptible *frisson* to any encounter.
3   Know when to turn it up and when to turn it down.
4   Stay juicy, vibrant, ready – and above all, stay *you*!

You are a sexual being – enjoy it!

OUTSIDE *part two*

CHAPTER 9

GIVING OUT THE *glow*

As you've probably realized, all the work you have been doing on yourself on the inside is going to pay dividends when you start to connect with people on the outside. When you can radiate and spread that inner glow to other people, you can begin to develop a deep energetic rapport and your connections will be more fun and more rewarding.

EYE CONTACT

As he took off his sunglasses he locked his deep blue eyes onto hers. As his pupils dilated, she felt a jolt of electricity run through her and took in a deep breath . . . She noticed his full soft lips part as his face creased into a wide, slightly crooked, sensual smile. It was as if they were suspended in time with a current zapping between them back and forth and in that instant, she felt herself smile back as her own lips parted and she breathed in the scent of him. She knew utterly and absolutely from deep inside herself that she wanted him.

When eyes meet, a spark is ignited which can be put out instantly or fanned into a fiercely burning fire. Eye contact is such an important part of the mating ritual that humans are almost the only primates that have the facility to mate face to face.

Eye contact is not just a wonderful way of signalling to a potential mate that you are interested, though, it is a prerequisite for human communication. Try the following exploration with a friend.

EYE TO EYE

- ♥ Look into each other's eyes and keep the contact for as long as possible. Time it if you can.
- ♥ When you do break off, check what thoughts and feelings you experienced.
- ♥ Who broke contact first or was it simultaneous?
- ♥ Share what happened with each other.

You may have felt uncomfortable or you may have felt a deepening of your relationship. Either way, the chances are you felt some strong emotion.

Our eyes are one of our most powerful signalling mechanisms. If you are going to connect successfully with someone, whether it is romantic or social, you have to make eye contact.

MIKE'S STORY: *Making Eye Contact*

Mike wrote this a few days after attending a flirting weekend:

Before, I tended to look straight down at the pavement when I noticed people approaching me. Today I was feeling so good I just looked straight ahead and felt completely at ease with myself.

Because I was in such a happy and unusually talkative mood when I got in the office I greeted a person I had never spoken to in my life.

Once Mike felt good and learned to use his eyes as a connection mechanism, he got results.

MORE EYE CONTACT

If, like Mike, you tend to look away from people rather than make eye contact, I invite you to try this out.

When you are walking down the street next time (in a safe, busy, daylight environment if you are a woman), try making eye contact with as many people as possible. Set yourself a target of three a day and build it up by one more each day.

When you notice someone you like, force yourself to make eye contact. You can easily walk away, but just get into the habit of looking at people you like. You'd be surprised how many people tell me that they avoid eye contact with people they are attracted to and end up flirting with people they aren't interested in!

Notice what happens when you make eye contact and how you feel. If you feel uncomfortable, good, keep at it, you are on the verge of feeling better. If you feel good, excellent, do more of it!

SURVEYING THE SCENE

We know that deep eye contact can convey deep feelings, but that's not always immediately appropriate. I'm sure you've been in situations where you needed to have a look round and survey the scene before making a move, with your eyes or otherwise! Here are a few ways to do this elegantly and quietly.

❤ When you want to survey a room, try looking just at the top of people's heads. You will get a peripheral view of everyone and they won't know you're looking at them in particular.

- When you want to survey an individual, imagine there is a circle round their face and run your eyes round the edge of that circle. You won't be making eye contact directly and they won't know what you're up to.
- You can also defocus your eyes and look behind someone, which enables you to get an impression of them without making direct eye contact.

TAKING IT FURTHER

When you spot someone you want to get friendlier with, you can use longer eye contact with a smile to say, 'Hi, hello, I'm here.' Even longer eye contact says, 'Hi, hello, I'm here, I'm interested!' A few repeated eye contacts will drive the message home!

If you don't get a positive response, never mind – someone out there is waiting for your glow to settle on them, so keep at it.

Try out all these suggestions next time you are in a crowd of people. You can do these on the train or bus, at work or a bar – anywhere.

THE SMILE

Eye contact is a vital communication opener, but eye contact coupled with a smile is an even more powerful flirting tool.

I bet you've been captivated when a baby smiles that wide smile of innocence and expectation. Maybe you've melted under the smile of a lover. Perhaps a chance smile has led to a conversation. Sometimes a smile bestowed on someone can change the focus of an entire day for that person.

SMILING ON THE INSIDE

A smile has to start on the inside. Remembering yourself at your best is a great prelude to a smile.

Try this for a moment:

- Check how you feel in your body right now.
- Turn up the corners of your mouth and fake a smile.
- Check how your body feels when you are smiling.

How many times a day do you smile to yourself at something? Why not do more of it? Smiling releases endorphins, nature's happy drugs. When you smile, you feel great!

SMILING AT STRANGERS

The only way you are going to notice the difference a random smile makes is to try it out yourself. You can do this next time you are walking down a street full of people.

Decide that you are going to do it, remember how you feel at your best and smile to yourself.

As someone approaches you, look at them, keep looking, make swift eye contact, then smile as you think nice thoughts.

You won't always get a positive response. This is OK. If you or they are wearing sunglasses, the likelihood of getting a smile acknowledged is slim, because you can't see each other's eyes. It may be that the person isn't used to it. They may be having a 'bad hair day' or worse. You won't know why they are rejecting your smile, but you will know it's *their* choice. Remember, if you get a 'no', go on to the next! You'll get a 'yes' eventually!

THE BEST CHAT-UP LINE

When people ask me for great chat-up lines, I always reply that the best is simply 'Hello' or 'Hi.' With your initial contact, you will communicate more through the way you feel and the energy you exude than through any fancy words you can come up with. If chat-up lines work, it's usually because the people using them feel great enough about themselves to take the risk. They are their own lines. You can be, too. You don't need anything else.

PETA'S STORY: *Connecting with Strangers*

When I run along the seafront where I live, I often see people coming towards me. If I am in the mood, I will focus on someone from afar and as they approach me, make eye contact. When that is held, I smile and say immediately, 'Hi' or

'Hello.' I rarely get a rebuff and if I do, I think, 'Maybe it's a bad hair day' or 'I don't know what just happened to them and I wish them well' or 'Maybe they were just surprised as they weren't used to it.'

It's easy when you feel good about yourself. My advice to you is to try it out.

STRANGERS ARE HUMAN TOO

You see strangers everywhere – on the train, in the street, at parties, in shops, pubs, bars. Why not smile and speak to them for no good reason? Start with the easy ones. Make eye contact and smile at the supermarket checkout person or a senior citizen in the queue. Many senior citizens live alone and welcome the contact. Perhaps you work in a large office or building. How many of your co-workers have you talked to? If it's only those you have to communicate with in the course of your work, now is a good time to start expanding your contacts. If you see someone with a child or a dog, smile and say hello to the child or dog first then look at the owner and smile. People seem to respond more easily to a positive interaction with their loved ones!

Not only is this a nice thing to do, but when you do it, you'll be surprised at the glow you get back. It will make you glow even more. Believe me, the glow is a gift you have to give. And although not everyone will accept your gift, someone, somewhere will appreciate it and you will have the pleasure of knowing you made someone feel good, if only for a tiny moment. And who knows who that person will smile at and who in turn they will smile at? You could be having a major effect on the state of the world!

But the main reason for doing this is that once you have developed the habit of making eye contact, smiling and saying hello to people, you will do it more naturally and then when that time comes when you really want to make an impression on someone, you will find yourself doing it easily and with a big smile on your face!

COMPLIMENTS – GIFTS FROM THE HEART

A genuine compliment costs nothing and it can light up someone's life. And once you make a person feel good, they'll want to spend more time with you!

A compliment is a gift you have to offer – give generously and genuinely.

When you feel good and are being yourself and your senses are open to what is around you and you have a belief that you are great, you will find reasons to compliment people everywhere. You might say you like them, appreciate their help, admire their sense of humour, delight in their company, enjoy making love to them – anything!

Many people hold back from giving compliments and in my view this is unnatural. It's like buying a present for someone and not giving it, except you don't have to buy compliments, there's an endless free store inside you. When I like someone or something about them, I tell them and this applies to friends, lovers and strangers. You can begin to do it too. Here are some of the things I have said to people:

'I like your independent spirit.'

'I love the way you smile.'

'You've got such a lovely energy.'

'You are so interesting.'

'Great skates!'

'What a lovely dog you have.'

'When I am with you I have so much fun.'

'I appreciate your honest and frank approach to life.'

'I was touched by the way you offered to help that person/dog/cat.'

'I admire the way you face challenges.'

'The words you wrote were poetic.'

'You are so good at [whatever it is they are good at].'

'You are such a good listener, thanks!'

Remember, these are things I say to people because that's who I am. You will find the right compliment to give to someone just by noticing them and being yourself.

Carol-Ann told me that she often thought of great compliments to give, she just never said them! When she tried letting them out, she got great responses most of the time!

You can find many things to say to many people when you see them not as something to be feared but as vulnerable and open beings like yourself who have beliefs, ideas, dreams and hopes – and who have endless wonders waiting to be unfolded.

If you don't get a great response, it's OK. If they laugh or brush it off, the compliment may not resonate with them or more likely they just don't know how to accept compliments. If that's the case, get them a copy of this book – they probably need help!

FINDING THE COMPLIMENT

- 💜 Make a list of all the people you know and like.
- 💜 Write next to each person's name the compliments you want to give them but haven't yet.
- 💜 Start giving the compliments!
- 💜 You must genuinely believe them to be true.

To help you, next time you find yourself in a group of new people, quickly look around and focus on things you like about the people around you. This way you are building up an instant stock of compliments. And just thinking about them will make it easier to say them.

RECEIVING COMPLIMENTS

If you get a genuine compliment, doesn't it make sense to take it to heart? So how come we are so good at taking rejection to heart yet we tend to brush compliments over our shoulder?

Sonya was wearing her brand new violet dress. James remarked how lovely she looked and how the colour suited her skin. Sonya turned to James and said, 'Oh this, it's just something I picked up. It's nothing special!' James was taken aback. Inside he was thinking, 'Whoa! I was just trying to be nice. That's the last time I pay her a compliment.'

When you brush off a compliment it is like ignoring a gift. If someone gives you a gift, do you put it aside and say things like 'You shouldn't have gone to so much trouble' or do you unwrap it in front of them and express your delight fully – if not in the gift, in the thought?

Learn to accept a compliment with the grace and good feelings with which it was given. People who give genuine compliments do so because they appreciate something about you. So be proud of who you are and be proud that people are paying you compliments. You must be giving off something nice!

Some good ways to receive compliments:

- 'Thank you, how nice of you to notice.'
- 'Thank you, it's one of my favourites.'
- 'Thank you, you've made my day.'

There are endless ways to receive a compliment, but it should always start with a smile and the words *'Thank you!'*

SUNSHINER VS. BLACK-CLOUDER

Imagine this scenario . . . Chris arrives at a party. He's late because someone at the office asked him to help out with a last minute emergency and he took ages to find a parking space. When he gets to the drinks table he finds all the red wine is gone and there's only beer left. He sees Jen coming towards him. She's a friend of the hostess, Anthea, and Chris has fancied Jen since meeting her at Anthea's housewarming party.

Jen raises her glass to Chris, smiles and says, 'Hi, how are you?'

'Huh?' grumbled Chris. 'I only just got here and haven't even got a drink yet. The red always goes first. And I hate beer, especially that cheap stuff they always get here. God, I've been so busy at work, it never stops, people wanting things all day long. And to cap it all, you know that book I ordered on how to sue and win? I waited seven days for it to arrive and they sent me the wrong one . . . Who are these people, morons?' As he paused for breath he looked up and Jen was gone.

Now imagine this scenario . . . Chris looks up and smiles. 'I was just thinking that it's probably a good thing all the red wine has gone. I'm not that keen on beer, so I'll stick to orange juice and that means I can drive instead of staying the night on the sofa. That reminds me of Anthea's last party. It was a good laugh, wasn't it?'

Chris makes eye contact with Jen, reaches out his hand as if to touch her and smiles. Jen smiles back.

'Do you know,' Chris continues, 'as I was leaving the office today someone asked me to sort out a problem? I was worried about being late, but that's silly, isn't it? I'm having a great time now. Do you want a lift home later?'

Same circumstances, different reaction. The scenario isn't real, but the way Chris reacts is based on real people. Life happens and we can choose our course of action and how we are in the world.

ARE YOU A SUNSHINER?

I call people who give out the glow 'sunshiners'. In the second scenario Chris is being a sunshiner. How do you react to life's challenges? Are you a sunshiner or a 'black-clouder'?

- ❤ Sunshiners look on the bright side.
- ❤ Sunshiners see the funny side of things.
- ❤ Sunshiners see people as opportunities.
- ❤ Sunshiners notice what's good about others and tell them.
- ❤ Sunshiners face challenges with: 'How can I move on?' or 'What can I learn here?'

- Sunshiners spend most of their time being who they are and loving it.
- Sunshiners only notice the possibilities.

When you choose the sunshine path, you'll find yourself giving out the glow of your own sunshine and that's one of the essentials of successful flirting.

CHAPTER 10

DEEP RAPPORT
—a natural state

Have you ever experienced a situation where you just seemed to hit it off with someone and the interaction flowed? You might also have had moments when you just couldn't seem to relate to someone. If you do get on with someone very easily, the chances are you have a deep natural rapport with them.

How much more powerful will a flirtatious encounter be if you can discover ways of creating a deep rapport in situations where it might not happen naturally?

WHAT DO I MEAN BY 'RAPPORT'?

Rapport is defined in the dictionary as 'a harmonious social interaction'. I see it as a dance between two or even more people with a flow of communication both verbally and non-verbally. It is also a shared rhythm and way of moving.

THE STRUCTURE OF RAPPORT

You've probably seen two people together and got a sense that they are really hitting it off. When you know what it is that they are doing, you can learn to do it, too, and get amazing results.

What is it that happens when two people are 'in rapport'?

♥ They may be facing each other with a degree of symmetry (hand matching hand, head matching head, knees matching feet).

♥ When one moves, the other may shift too.

♥ When one laughs, the other may laugh too.

♥ When one looks the other in the eyes, the other looks back.

♥ They may be breathing symmetrically.

♥ They will almost certainly be moving at the same pace and with a similar rhythm.

♥ Their energy will be matched (i.e., one will not be moving around rapidly and shouting loudly while the other is quiet and moving slowly).

♥ They may be reflecting back each other's language.

Whether they are lovers or not, these two people may be unconsciously enacting a deep-seated primordial form of mating dance. Animals and birds throughout the world perform symmetrical and synchronized harmonious mating dances, and when people are attracted to each other, they begin to synchronize with each other automatically.

This type of activity is not limited to lovers. People who are locked in harmonious discussion, whether it is business or social, will often naturally assume each other's postures as they begin to agree more and more.

You may have heard of things like 'matching' and 'mirroring', where someone consciously mirrors another's posture. These are rather *passé* techniques for gaining rapport. The success of this technique depends to some extent on people not knowing about it and on doing it very elegantly. Now that this is common knowledge, people are on the look out for it and may feel uncomfortable by having their actions copied.

There are many other more powerful and subtle ways of making people feel comfortable with you and gaining a deep rapport so that it happens naturally rather than in a manufactured way. You can practise this deeper form of rapport with anyone and begin to create instant harmony and accord.

I don't think I have to remind you how much that will help you in your social, professional and romantic interactions, do I?

Create Only Good Magic

Before we start, a word of warning. Some people have tried using rapport skills to manipulate people in ways that are not useful to them or others. This might work initially, but it will also wear off quickly and when it does, the people who were manipulated will not like whoever tried it and in the end that person will feel bad as well. And I know you only want to influence others by making them feel good.

THE MAGIC OF DEEP RAPPORT

Deep rapport goes beyond moving your hands to the same position as another person or crossing your legs when they do. It isn't about deliberately mimicking another person, although these skills can be useful when done elegantly. Deep rapport goes beyond the individual movements to the whole body sense that lies behind them.

AWARENESS IS ALL

All of us, whether or not we are warriors, have a cubic centimetre of chance that pops up in front of our eyes from time to time. The difference between the average man and the warrior is that the warrior is aware of this and one of his tasks is to be alert, deliberately waiting, so that when the cubic centimetre pops up, he'll have the necessary speed and prowess to pick it up.

Carlos Castaneda

People are giving you information every second you are with them, even from across a room. Like a warrior you need to be alert to what is going on and be ready to act rapidly when you get the signal.

As you start to really notice people, you will begin to pick up on the unique things they do.

- ❤ You will notice how they move and use their hands.
- ❤ You will notice how they change their physiology to match their mood.
- ❤ You will notice where they look when they feel good.

- 💜 You will notice the rate of and changes in their breathing.
- 💜 You will realize that when people do these things they are giving you a holographic map of their experience. What treasures do you think a map like that might show to you?

The two most powerful ways to gain rapport with someone are to breathe at the same rate as them and to match their energy levels. Naturally I don't advise you do this with someone who is very depressed, drunk or out of control!

MATCHING BREATHING

You know how an animal sniffs out the air, opening its nostrils and parting its lips, checking out the sounds and smells? You can do all this and more. You can notice many things through your peripheral vision and you can catch the rise and fall of someone's breathing and allow yourself to just fall into the same rhythm and breathe along with them. . .

BREATHE. . .

Try this on the train. Pick someone to experiment with and look around (not directly at) their shoulders and upper chest. You will probably notice the rise and fall of their jacket or their shoulders. This is a clue to their breathing rate. Keeping your eyes on the breathing cues, start breathing in time with them.

Matching breathing is probably the most powerful aid to deepening an encounter with someone. It's so powerful that it is one of the basic building blocks of tantric sex! But when you do this exploration with strangers, nothing will happen unless you decide to make eye contact and interact with them. It's entirely safe!

SENSING THEIR ENERGY

You know that everyone has different energy levels. If you can match someone's energy comfortably, you will gain instant rapport with them.

So, before you approach a person, watch them for a while and notice how they move. People show their energy levels in the way they move. The elements are a great metaphor for different levels of movement and energy. You may remember we explored them earlier.

Before you approach someone, take some time to watch them and notice how they move. Ask yourself these questions as you watch them:

- Are their movements rapid, jerky and fire-like?
- Are they rhythmical, flowing and watery?
- Are they speedy, light and airy?
- Are they solid, slow and earthy?

If you have a chance to listen to them talk, notice the energetic quality of their conversation.

- Do they talk in staccato, piercing rapid-fire tones?
- Does their conversation seem to flow, rising and falling at an even pace?
- Are they waving their hands around in the air and talking fast?
- Are they talking slowly and deliberately?

SHIFTING INTO SOMEONE'S ENERGY LEVEL

Remember how you can shift into different ways of moving? (If you don't, go back and do the exploration on page 103.)

As you watch someone, imagine yourself making similar movements. This is a form of mental rehearsal. It makes it easy to just take on someone else's movement pattern.

Slowly, ease your body into the sense of the person's movement and get a sense of their rhythm and their flow. It's like tapping your fingers to a beat, only you're doing it with your whole body.

When you get a sense of their rhythm and begin to synchronize with them, you will have already established deep rapport without saying a word and you will be in a position to lead them to a level that is right for both of you.

ENGAGING FURTHER

As you get into someone else's rhythm, you may find it difficult to sustain it for any length of time. You can lead them to an in-between rhythm that suits both of you.

The way to do it is match their rhythm, then begin to speed up or slow down in small increments. You will magically find them moving with you. The idea is to find a pace that is right for both of you.

If you are in a close relationship with someone you have trouble getting on with, check whether your rhythms are very different. You might be able to improve the situation with a little deep rhythm rapport!

TONAL RAPPORT

One of the greatest ways to get into synch with someone is to match their tone or speed of voice.

As I am listening to someone's first sentence in my head I am replicating their tone and speed. Then, when I match that tone and speed in my reply, it doesn't sound like mimicry, I just sound like them. They feel comfortable because you sound familiar.

You can practise this on the telephone. Each time the phone rings, let it be a trigger to you to go into listening mode, opening up those sharp senses.

You can start by just noticing the speed of the voice and then matching it. If they are talking too fast or too slowly for you, once you have matched their level, you can gently slow down or speed up a little. Continue to do this, going back to their level if necessary and coming down or up in smaller increments until you notice that they are beginning follow you. Provided you do it at a comfortable pace, bit by bit, you will be able to bring them and yourself to a mid level that is comfortable for *both* of you.

What happens is that when you are matching a person at their level they feel comfortable and like you, because people like people who are like themselves. They are then much more inclined to follow you and you can be more natural without straining to be just like them.

This is one of the basic tools of good hypnotists. I use this method all the time to get my clients relaxed and open them to suggestion. What you will be doing is exactly the same. I bet you didn't realize how easy it is! Practise this as often as you can and you will find in time that it becomes a natural part of your conversational style.

SPATIAL RAPPORT

When you enter someone's personal space you might do so as a welcome guest or an alien invader or a bold visitor who believes they can just pop in. . . Are you a space invader?

As you stand and talk to people every day in the normal course of your life, begin to notice the 'language' of space.

- When you get close, do they move backwards, even minutely?
- Are they trying to change sides all the time?
- Do they start to fidget as you get closer?
- Do they contract a bit, bringing their arms in or crossing their arms?
- Do they put their hands up as if to push you away?

These are all signs that you are too close.

Before you blunder in you've got to learn to case the space.

CASING THE SPACE

Ask a few good friends, men and women, to let you try this exploration out with them. Tell them the truth – that you are finding out about personal space and you want to know how close is too close. Would they mind standing there and letting you come closer? They can tell you when to stop. They'll probably be secretly fascinated and want to give it a go themselves.

Best to do this when sober!

- Start out about 8 feet away from your friend.
- Start to approach them naturally. Keep alert and watch out for any changes such as muscles twitching, eyes blinking, breathing changing or skin colour altering. Keep getting closer until they stop you!
- Ask them to help you out by checking a few reactions. Go to a spot where you thought you noticed a change in the person. Ask them if they feel anything there.
- Move to the next spot where you felt them change. Ask them again. If your feelings don't match up, it's OK. You are just learning.
- Ask them to tell you where you got too close.
- And what it feels like when you are too close.

Everyone will have their own limits. Remember friends will feel more comfortable being close to you than strangers will.

When you approach strangers, remember to case their space. If you are noticing some reaction but aren't sure what it means, you can always ask: 'Are you comfortable with me standing here?' or 'Is it OK if I stand here?' They will respect you for asking.

FORGET THE CHAT UP AND MAKE THEM CHAT

One of the things people in my classes always complain about is that they don't know what to say. They've got it the wrong way round. Great flirts don't depend on clever chat-up lines or having something meaningful to say. They depend on their ability to get people to open out and talk. Everyone loves to talk about themselves. Great flirts are experts in make-'em-chat lines!

We've already covered the greatest chat-up line of all. 'Hello', 'Hi' or 'Good morning' all work perfectly well.

Once you have said that and before you take the flirtation further, wouldn't it be useful to find out as much information as possible about someone? After all, they may not be right for you! This doesn't just apply to romantic situations, but to any conversation you might have with someone you don't know. If you've ever been stuck when making small talk at conferences or social gatherings, this might be of benefit to you.

The greatest questions you can ask are ones that lead someone to remember a positive experience. You could start by offering a short sentence on how you like to have fun, relax, etc, and then ask them. . .

- 'What's your ideal way to have fun?'
- 'If you could wake up tomorrow and have it all, what would your ideal day be like?'
- 'How do you like to relax?'
- 'Tell me about your best holiday ever.'
- 'What are you passionate about?'

As you listen to the answers, be alert for the clues mentioned above. These clues tell you how people structure their world and you can use them to build up a multi-dimensional map of a person.

The more you practise this, the more natural it becomes. Be observant. The key is to ask a question that will get a person to access positive experiences and pay attention.

THEY HAND IT TO YOU ON A PLATE

As they talk, people move their hands and mark out certain things with gestures. As you listen to someone and notice these gestures, you are already constructing their map in your head.

When you get a map of people's linked gestures and language, you can refer back to it. For example, if someone is talking about a time when they were in love and you notice that in connection with that they keep making a certain gesture in a certain place in the space around them, you can refer back to that time and at the same time, look at or point to the space they marked out. They will instantly recognize that you have understood their world. Your gesture will also connect them back more deeply to the feeling of being in love. And might endear you to them. . .

THEY DIRECT YOU TO IT

When people are accessing certain memories, they will rest their gaze in specific directions. They will look in completely different directions depending on whether they are accessing bad memories or good ones. As with their hand movements, you can get them to access their positive memories by looking where they look as you talk.

For example, 'So, that time you won the championship [look in the direction they looked in], how did that feel?'

Once again they will feel a deep connection with you and sense that you are in their flow.

And then, if you want, you can take it further. . .

SEXUAL RAPPORT

If you want it, this is how to go for it!

When you are with someone and you want them, let them know from the inside out.

Girls, you can do this easily. You can signal it. Just be sure you know what you want, then go for it – and be honest and proud of it and *be careful!*

Guys, be careful too. Wait for the clues, watch for the signs. Women are notorious for giving out mixed signals. The more alert you are, the more you are going to notice those little shifts in a person that either warn you to take care or invite you to go for it. Use this wisely.

If you want to gain sexual rapport with someone, just use the juice – shake it up and pour it out!

❤ Do the sexual breathing exercise *(see page 122)*. Start generating the sexual waves.

❤ Breathe into the experience – your breathing will change and the other person will notice it unconsciously.

- ♥ Move closer to the person.
- ♥ Flare your nostrils and breathe in their scent.
- ♥ Gently expand and thrust out your chest/breasts, slowly and as you breathe.
- ♥ Imagine sending out with each breath a wave of your energy and your scent directly into the other person.
- ♥ Look them in the eye, breathe in time with them and say to yourself the words you want to say to them.
- ♥ Continue to do this until you get a response. (At all times remain alert for any signals that they want you to back off. If you get these signals, stop! What are these signals? If you have been studying people as suggested in 'Sharpen Up your Senses' and you have practised the explorations on checking out personal space, you'll probably have an idea of what happens when people are trying to move away from you.)
- ♥ Gauging your way and paying attention, you can move in closer and closer on each positive response – maybe a sigh or the beginning of a smile or something more obvious.
- ♥ Enjoy it and make sure they enjoy it too!

DEEP RAPPORT – BUBBLING UP

When you enter the dance and go with the flow and the rhythm, whether in a group of people or with someone you desire, you will begin to be able to incorporate all this into your own potent mixture of who you are at your best, mingling and communicating with other people, glowing as you dance the dance of deep rapport, drawing them closer to you.

And like that, wouldn't it be great to be able to generate luscious ways of talking so that people feel even more attracted to you and your ideas? That's next on the agenda!

CHAPTER 11

LUSCIOUS *language*

LANGUAGE: AN EXQUISITE POWER

Language is a powerful tool. Many of us have found this out the hard way. You can alienate people by using words indiscriminately and miss opportunities to connect by using *your* language instead of picking up on *theirs*. Worst of all, you can talk people into very unproductive states, like Jeff did, quite unconsciously.

JEFF'S STORY: *A Grim State of Affairs*

Jeff plucked up the courage to ask a girl out on a date. This is what he said: 'Er, um, Jeff here, you probably don't remember me, but we met at Joanne's party. You're probably too busy, but I was wondering if you'd like to come out sometime. I don't suppose you'd want to. No? Okay!'

Jeff's chances of getting a date with this are slim unless he happens to appeal to someone's sympathetic mothering instincts, but he's looking for a girlfriend, *not* a mother! Jeff's language is suggesting to the girl that:

A   She won't remember him.

B   She'll be busy.

C   She won't want to come out.

D   She'll say, 'No.'

His language is hypnotic, but instead of being persuasive it's rather dissuasive!

In this chapter, you will find ways to use language so that the person you are communicating with is more likely to go along with your suggestions. This is *not* about persuading someone against their will, it *is* about making sure that your language assists rather than hinders you in seeking the co-operation of others.

Great flirts always use language that creates a good feeling in others and thus makes them more likely to agree with them. This isn't about saying 'You *would* want to come out with me, wouldn't you?' It's much more subtle, as you will find out.

Meantime, I invite you to monitor the language you use and hear every day. Check out how often you and others make negative suggestions that could encourage someone to say 'no' when you want them to say 'yes'! As you read through this chapter, you will find that most of the language patterns I talk about can be used to create either negative or positive suggestions. Language is powerfully persuasive stuff!

LANGUAGE: THE PERSUASION GAME

When you learn to use it exquisitely, you can really charm and influence people with your language:

- ❤ You can guide and motivate people to make useful choices.
- ❤ You can clarify a person's meaning as well as show you care about and are interested in them.
- ❤ You can match the way someone senses the world, making them feel comfortable with you.

All good flirts do this naturally! But the secret lies in guiding rather than forcing. You cannot make people do something that goes against their own values. You will alienate them if you try.

In the end people make their own choices and they have the right to say 'yes' *or* 'no'. Fortunately, you know that everyone has this right and that you respect it. Be a guide, not a manipulator.

The best persuader is one who believes that their role is to help people make decisions that are right for them.

The keys to being a persuasive linguist are as follows:

- Be you at your best. Wizards of linguistic influence get their best results when they are in a positive and upbeat state of mind.
- Know the purpose and direction of your communication. What do you want to have happen?
- Do you want to get someone to agree to do something?
- Do you want to start a conversation with someone so that you can discover whether you want to continue?
- How do you want the person to feel as a result of communicating with you?

- Gain deep energetic rapport with someone. In fact this is a precursor to opening your mouth.
- Establish verbal contact. 'Hi' or 'Hello' are the best words to start with.
- Be clear about the emotions and states you want others to experience so that your suggestions can take root. Work out the sequence you want them to experience them in. For example, do you want them to be curious first, then excited, then convinced about your idea?

When you are thinking of persuading or influencing anyone to do something it might be useful to bear the following in mind:

- How useful will it be to gain knowledge of their preferences in terms of needs, desires and wants?
- How useful will it be to find what did or didn't work for them in the past?
- How useful will it be to find out what's important to them?
- If you already know the person, what answers do you have to those questions and what other information do you need that will help you influence them?

'YOU'RE SO AGREE-ABLE'

Now, before you do anything else, take a moment to read this sentence:

You are reading this book, the book has pages, and on each page are lines of print, and on each line are words, made up of characters.

You may be nodding or agreeing with me because I just said things that absolutely had to be true. This is a technique that is used widely in hypnosis and by the world's top persuaders to get a person into an 'agree-able' frame of mind. You do this by making simple statements they just have to agree with!

Salespeople use it all the time. They say things like:

- 'You want value for money.'
- 'You want to go home knowing you've bought the right car/house/dress.'

Great flirts use it all the time. They say things like:

- 'My, it's busy in here.'
- 'Have you noticed how many people are dancing in here?'
- 'I notice you are drinking [whatever it is].'

Later, when the conversation goes further, SuccessFlirts use 'Yes, that's true' statements like the ones below to get people into a good state of mind:

- 'You want to feel good, don't you?'
- 'I bet you want to enjoy your life.'
- 'I'm sure you want to be happy.'
- 'You like being with people like you.'

Because the other person has to agree with such statements, they get into 'yes mode'. And when they are in an 'agree-able' state, how much more likely that they are going *to agree* with your next suggestion – the important one. How useful to your love life, career and friendships would it be to get people into an 'agree-able' state?

FINDING 'YES, THAT'S TRUE' STATEMENTS

Get used to creating statements that induce people into saying 'yes', whether though nodding their head, smiling, making a sound or actually saying, 'Yes, that's true!'

Take any situation – the office, the train, a restaurant, a bar – and find as many agreeable points as you can. For example, if you are in a restaurant, look around at people and find things that could apply to all of them, things they would agree with if you were to suggest them to them.

To exercise the muscle start with obvious and refine it:

- 'You are eating at this restaurant.'
- 'You looked at the menu.'
- 'You are drinking red wine.'

Getting people into the habit of saying 'yes' could be very useful when asking someone for a date or trying to persuade someone to go with an idea.

THE VAGUE REFERENCE
They Are Doing It to You

Politicians, advertisers and newspapers use vague language to persuade and influence you all the time. Cola adverts refer to their product as 'the real thing'. Politicians talk about 'building an education system in which all children are educated to the highest standards that can be reasonably expected'. A tampon manufacturer uses the word 'freedom' in association with its product.

What do these words mean to you?:

- confidence
- a life that works
- happiness
- a fulfilling relationship

Just for fun ask your friends what they mean to them. You'll find everyone has their own meaning and that they will generally be positive meanings.

Because the words and statements in advertising campaigns are so vague but generally associated with positive things, a person has to fill in the blanks with their own experience to make meaning out of them. So they don't feel coerced and certain emotions can be generated in them without the risk of getting too specific and 'mis-matching' their experience. People think they know what is meant and, what's more, link the good feelings to the person speaking or the particular product being advertised!

How useful would it be for you to link a person's own specific positive feelings to you?!

LINKING POSITIVE FEELINGS

Super seducers and great flirts do this all the time, using statements such as:

- 'Can you imagine what it is like to relax and really enjoy just passing time with someone you like?'
- 'What's it like when you get that sense of just wanting to let go?'

- 'There are things you long for in your life, we all do.'
- 'How do you know when something has really fulfilled you?'
- 'You've had that sense of satisfaction before – you know, when you've completed something or done something well?'
- 'You know that feeling of meeting someone and thinking you've known them all your life?'
- 'You know how when you get that laid-back feeling and just want to relax. . .?'
- 'You know those times when you've just clicked with someone and experienced a deep sense of connection?'
- 'I don't know about you, but there are some things in life that I find so exciting.'
- 'You know what it's like when you are really curious about something and can't wait to find out?'

Using this language generates the desired state in people and opens them up to your ideas. As they get into the state, you can link yourself to them, just as 'natural' is linked to the advertiser's product.

One great motivational speaker does this linking all the time. He gets people into really strong states and thumps his fist on his chest as he does it. As you go into the state, you remember him pounding his chest. He is linked into that state. He even talks about God and points to himself. Believe me, this is very powerful stuff. This particular person has managed to arouse guru-like adoration by using these skills in this way. This is not what I am suggesting to you, but some of the rapid seduction trainers out there are teaching this technique to men with some success. They talk to women about getting a 'deep sense of connection with someone' and about 'being relaxed'. Think how much more receptive you might be to another person's overtures when you are curious and relaxed.

One friend of mine learnt how to do handwriting analysis and uses it as a flirting technique. He does it in restaurants with waitresses. When the waitress takes the order he looks at her, smiles and in a very relaxing and slightly naughty voice he asks to see her pad. He then says, with a smile, 'Oh dear, what a pity there's not enough.' Curiosity aroused, she asks, 'What do you mean?' He says, 'I do handwriting analysis and it's pretty powerful, but there's not enough here to tell you, etc.' She's drawn into his world and it's much easier for him to strike up a conversation and make a move if he wants to.

The lesson here is not how to use techniques to flirt, but to realize that when you arouse someone's curiosity and speak to them in a relaxing voice you draw them in and they are more open to your suggestions!

You might like to try this exploration.

CREATE YOUR OWN VAGUE SUGGESTION PATTERNS

- ♥ Think of some situations where this would be useful for you.
- ♥ Think of some states you would like to create in people and how they would help you.
- ♥ Create some sentences that you could use.

You could start with some 'agreeable' phrases and as you continue add in phrases that convey the statements on pages 36–38 and add in the states you want to create.

Try them out – the world is full of people to practise on! You may find yourself using them consciously at first, but it will become more natural as time goes on.

SENSE-ABLE LANGUAGE

You will remember that people use different types of language according to the way they structure the world. They also use a mixture of sense-based language based on the senses of sight, sound, feeling, smell and taste. (You might like to look back to pages 36–38 to remind yourself of the types of language people use.)

When you pay attention to people around you, you may find that some have a predominant sensory system they use when describing experience. Take the following three passages, for example. I am describing a walk to a beach.

In the distance behind me I could hear the wind whistling through the trees. A twig cracked and I heard my soft footfall on the ground beneath me as I walked along.

As we approached the beach, leaving the road and the sounds of traffic, I could hear the whoosh of the waves interspersed with the cry of sea birds. And when I stood on the shore, listening to the waves breaking rhythmically in front of me, I thought, 'This place really resonates with me.'

In the distance behind me rose the tall pine trees with their dark green needles. The sky was a bright cloudless blue and the earth was a rich red, scattered with lighter pebbles and stones and bushes of every hue of Mediterranean green.

As we approached the beach, I could see the sun shimmering on the water. The deep turquoise blue of the sea was shot through with flecks of white spume. And when I stood on the white sandy beach, I thought, 'This place is brilliant.'

I could feel the sharp but stimulating carpet of pine needles under my feet as the breeze blew from between the trees across my head. I felt the intermittent warmth of the sun as it forced its way through the fragile canopy of pines. It was warm and I sensed a coolness as the droplets of perspiration started to form on my forehead.

As I walked along the shore I could feel the grains of sand between my toes and the soft cushion of sand. As the cool water lapped my ankles, I thought to myself, 'This place feels so right.'

Which of those descriptions gave you the richest experience of that place? How much fuller was your sense of it when you had read all three? How would adding other senses like smell and taste enrich these descriptions?

Generally, people respond with varying levels of interest to descriptive language, depending on which sensory descriptions you use. Pay attention to what they prefer and when you get a sense of it, start using those kinds of words back to them. Great flirts instinctively pick up on other people's language and use it in their conversation so that the person they are engaging feels at home with them.

Better still – start developing rich sensory descriptions of your own so that you appeal to everyone!

STORYTELLING

All cultures use stories to get across a deeper message. Once you have got past the first encounter by saying 'Hi' or 'Hello', you can introduce stories into your conversation to get someone into a great state of mind and be more receptive to your flirting! For example:

'It's nearly Christmas. Funny how once a year people seem so disposed to be nicer and more accepting to each other. When you are like that, don't you think you're more generous, open and receptive to new ideas? I was offered a taste of a new cocktail at a party the other night and I was surprised how great something I don't normally drink can taste when it is part of a different mixture. It's kind of exciting.'

And isn't that a great story for getting a client to open out to an old idea in a new format, for example, or to set someone up for considering trying a new product or idea, or indeed to encourage someone to be open to you?

There's a story for every state of mind you want to generate and every message you want to convey. Start being aware of stories people tell and things that happen to you and you'll soon build up a mental reference library of great stories.

What situations would benefit from you using stories to get across a message? What stories can you tell to create the following states?:

- curiosity
- eagerness
- desire
- anticipation

Telling a story about something and keeping a person guessing might easily elicit curiosity. Telling a story about Christmas and waiting to open presents might elicit anticipation.

Look for stories that don't directly relate to the situation of the person you are talking to.

You can also tell other people's stories, for example, 'I remember someone telling me about this guy she knew. . .' That way you can convey a message without getting into deep trouble by telling lies! I call this 'the artfully-vague-memory storytelling method'.

PERSUASIVE LANGUAGE PATTERNS

READING SOMEONE'S MIND

When you use words like 'I know you are . . .', you are entering the realms of mind reading. Mind reading can be offensive, but it can also be very useful in leading someone to a better experience, for example:

- 'I know you like to enjoy yourself and I know that you've had some great experiences. . .'
- 'I am sure you are wondering how you know when someone is right for you.'

In the second example, your language will cause the listener to unconsciously check out how they do know if someone is right for them. And you are sending them on a destination of *your* choosing. Is this manipulation? Well, if they don't like it, they'll soon jump out and shake their heads.

YOU LIKE THIS, DON'T YOU?

Have you ever listened to any of those legal series on TV where you get a lot of courtroom action? You will have heard lawyers say things like:

- 'So, Mr Roberts, you wanted your mother out of the way, did you not?'
- 'And, Miss Johnson, I am sure you will agree that you were just a little bit angry at what happened, weren't you?'

These questions appear to be giving choice, but they are not. They are actually leading the person to a particular response.

Think what happens when someone says things to you like:

- 'It's interesting, reading this book, don't you think?'
- 'It's a great night for a walk in the park, isn't it?'
- 'I'm sure you would love to eat a great meal in fantastic surroundings, wouldn't you?'

You are making a statement and adding on a statement at the end that encourages them to agree with you. It makes it easier for them to go with the suggestion in the statement, wouldn't you agree? These 'tag' questions, as they are called, serve to reinforce the preceding statement.

Think how useful this might be in getting agreement from someone, be it in a romantically flirtatious situation or a professional conversation.

EMBEDDING THE IDEA

Stop. Don't **read** any **further** in this chapter unless there are things you want from other people that you haven't been able to achieve yet. Whether you think **you can** or not is irrelevant at this point in terms of what it takes you to **be effective** and use language **in extremely powerful ways**.

Hidden in the sentences above there are commands. They have been highlighted in bold. **Read further, you can be effective in powerful ways!** But before trying this out, remember that you can't compel someone to do something against their will, although you can lead them towards something that they might be open to.

When you change your tone of voice and make it more emphatic as you say the command words, and people are in a good state, and you have deep rapport, and you have a good rhythm, and you are pacing them and observing what is going on, they can unconsciously pick up on these commands. A lot of factors have to be in place before this works well. You can't do it without rapport, tonality and a good state.

HOW TO DO IT

To create an embedded command, you just have to place a command in a small sentence. To emphasize that it is a command, you need to understand the effect of tonality on the end of a sentence:

- ❤ If the tone goes up, people hear a question.
- ❤ If the tone stays the same, people hear a statement.
- ❤ If the tone goes down, people hear a command.

Good communicators use this tonality unconsciously.

In order to make the command more effective, say the first part of the sentence, pause and then change the tonality and make your voice louder as you say the command words.

One of my favourite embedded commands is the sentence: 'And so, you, **like me**, are aware of the good things this book is offering.'

Neat command, eh?

BEWARE OF BAD COMMANDS

How often do people say things like 'You shouldn't **feel bad**'? Most of us use these commands without realizing it. And sometimes, when someone is vulnerable and not feeling too good, the command can emphasize their state. Think before you speak! Now that you know what to listen out for, you can change it. Get used to doing it and you'll find yourself doing it unconsciously as you progress.

As you become more aware of this, you may also begin to notice how other people give out bad commands. If you spot any bad commands embedded in this book, let me know – constructive feedback is valuable to all of us!

NEGATIVES: DON'T READ THIS

Right, now don't think of having great sex. Don't think of what you had for breakfast. Don't read this.

I bet you did think of having great sex, even though the command was to not do so!

The negative is a curious phenomenon. In order for the brain to process it, it has to think first of the thing you are telling it not to think of in order to think of not doing it!

Sometimes this can be less than helpful. What's one of the most common things we say to people when we want to comfort them? 'Don't *worry*!' By using the word 'worry', we have drawn their attention to worry. Likewise, 'Don't *panic*!', a common phrase used when fires break out.

So, how often do you use words in this way and what effect might you be having on people? What other words could you use in these situations? 'Don't *panic*!' could become 'Stay *calm*.'

When using language to influence people, remember this golden rule:

Always use words that clarify what you *want* people to do or feel, not what you don't want them to do.

PRESUPPOSING MAKES IT SO

One of the most powerfully persuasive linguistic tools is the presupposition. Presuppositions are the things we assume to be so, without saying them. When we say, 'She was giving off the signs' for example, we are presupposing there was a woman and that there were signs and that she was sending those signs. Those elements have to be there for the sentence to make sense.

Have you seen those magazine articles that say things like: *'How much more exciting can your sex life get?'* These words come from a belief that presupposes that you have an exciting sex life and that it can get better.

Great flirts and influencers use this sort of thing all the time by setting up sentences that presuppose whatever it is they want you to agree with.

'How about getting together for a coffee on Wednesday or Saturday?' This presupposes you would like to get together and that it will be on one of two days. You are led to make a decision about Wednesday or Saturday, not about whether you want coffee or not!

Compare that with the unconscious response you might give to *'Would you like to come out with me sometime?'* This sentence leaves too much open!

Presuppositions are all about implanting the idea that something will happen and it's just a matter of how, when and in what way it will happen.

PRESUPPOSITIONS

Check out these sentences and work out what is being presupposed and how it might affect you. I'll do the first one for you:

'When would be a good time for us to meet for a drink – one day this week, or next weekend?'

This presupposes:

- ❤ You would like to meet me.
- ❤ You and I are going to meet.
- ❤ It will be for a drink.
- ❤ It will either be this week or next weekend.

Now check out these statements. What is being presupposed here?

- ❤ 'It doesn't matter whether you get back to me by e-mail or fax. I'll look forward to your answer.'
- ❤ 'Do you want to check out that new bar I told you about before or after the play?'
- ❤ 'How easy do you find it to relax after a busy day at the office?'
- ❤ 'Before you decide, think about how many useful contacts you could make at the party.'
- ❤ 'I'd like to go over a few points before you complete the project.'
- ❤ 'Have you noticed how effortless it is to sit back and just enjoy what's happening right now?'

The point of presuppositions as a persuasive language pattern is that you give the listener choices, but they all presuppose the response you want to get!

Using the above examples it might be useful to have a go at exercising your ability to generate presuppositions for those occasions when someone might benefit from a little prod in the decision-making process!

CREATING PRESUPPOSITIONS

Words like 'before, 'as', 'while' are all great words to use when creating presuppositions.

Read this sentence:

As you are sitting there and reading this, you may be wondering how easily you can learn to flirt successfully.

What did that do to you? Stop and think. With that little two letter word 'as' I am linking a fact that is true to something I want to suggest to you.

How can you put these things together to make magical suggestions to people?

Here are a few clues. Think of a state you want to create, for example curiosity. In that case you might say to someone:

- ❤ 'I don't know how curious you are when. . .'
- ❤ 'As soon as you get curious. . .'
- ❤ 'Before you become a little curious. . .'
- ❤ 'Do you feel very curious or just a little?'

There are loads of ways to do it. . .

Now go do it yourself!

CREATING PRESUPPOSITIONS

- ❤ Think of a future interaction you might want to have with someone – your boss, a friend, a romantic interest.
- ❤ Think about what would be useful to be presupposed. Do you want them to presuppose that something is easy, that they will greatly benefit from it, that they will really, really enjoy it?
- ❤ Write out statements with presuppositions that will guide people in that direction. Use the examples as guidelines. Write out as many as you feel will help – if you don't use them now, they will come in useful later.

PERSUADEE'S REMORSE

Sometimes these techniques seem to work perfectly because people are gullible and vulnerable and trust you. If you don't have their best interests at heart you may get results initially, but they will be accompanied by 'persuadee's remorse'.

PETA'S STORY: *A Flattering Persuasion*

An acquaintance called me to offer me a 'business opportunity'. She was trying to get me to attend an 'open evening' and eventually to join a network marketing programme. Normally I say 'no' to these things, but the conversation went something like this:

Hi, Peta! Something fascinating happened to me recently where I got to make a load of money easily. It got me thinking who is one of the most outgoing, curious and interesting people I know and could really benefit from this. And Peta, you came to mind. You always seem to have a knack of connecting with the right people. And that's why this business opportunity would be a doddle for you.

There's a free evening being held in London. Which day would you like to come, Wednesday or Saturday?

I went to that meeting and I got involved because I allowed myself to be led by the overpoweringly persuasive language of my friend, who at that time was much more skilled than me at this stuff! Later when I realized that in order to make money I'd have to use the same tactics on my friends, I opted out of the scheme. I felt as if my friend had conned me. I learned a lesson in taking responsibility for myself, but it took a long time before I felt comfortable about any suggestions that particular friend made to me.

So, when you use persuasive language, do try to be sure that what you are suggesting is right for the other person. Remember, be a guide, not a manipulator.

WITH THE RIGHT ATTITUDE, IT WORKS!

With the right attitude, however, these linguistic patterns can be powerful seduction tools. Ross Jeffries is an American expert on seduction. He didn't have much luck with women and developed his 'speed seduction' techniques to remedy this situation.

I have no intention of trying to replicate Ross's excellent work here, but the kind of work I do is a great precursor to what he teaches. If you want to pursue this further, check out Ross's material in the Resources section.

Meanwhile, think how you could begin to adapt these patterns to make people more attracted to you. Anything is possible!

LANGUAGE: THE EXPLORATION GAME

MAKING SENSE OF THEIR WORDS

Our words are the repositories of vast oceans of sensory information and experience. They mean something unique to us. We can all agree on words like 'dog' and 'cat'. But if I asked you to think of a cat, your picture would be very different from mine.

Because words contain a great deal of emotional attachment, it is respectful to honour them when talking to people.

PAUL'S STORY: *A Passionate 'Obsession'*

A friend of mine is a motorcycle journalist. When he isn't writing about bikes, he's testing new bikes, racing bikes or reading about bikes. When I first met him, I remarked, 'You are obsessed with bikes.' As I spoke I noticed his face change. He frowned slightly, his mouth tightened a fraction and he sat back. Something wasn't right.

Before he could reply, I asked him, 'What do *you* mean by "obsession"?'

He told me, 'I don't like that word to describe what I do. Obsession is too strong a word. Obsession is unhealthy. I am *passionate* about bikes but not obsessed with them".'

In this particular encounter, the word 'obsession' had quite positive connotations for me, but for him it meant something quite negative.

ARE YOU SAYING WHAT YOU MEAN?

The words we use have unique meaning for us. If we were to explain that meaning for every single word we use, we'd never get round to communicating, of course. Our language has patterns built in that allow us to speak more fluently. We tend to delete, generalize and sometimes distort our language. But sometimes people use language that is so vague that another person has to imagine what they mean. This is a serious block to clear and meaningful communication!

Fortunately there are ways of challenging vague statements to get more clarification. This is really useful in initial encounters. It's vital that we don't leave an interaction with the wrong idea. . .

QUESTIONING YOUR WAY TO CLARITY

Generalizations

Say, for example, someone tells you, 'I'm no good with people.' This person is making things appear much worse by using a generalized statement. To get clarification here, you can ask: 'Which people?' or 'I bet there's been an occasion when you've got along with someone, hasn't there?'

By challenging a statement in this way you can lead a person to a better state of mind. Remember, getting people into good states is essential if you want to have a positive interaction with them. This is a useful technique to use in a friendship or business situation, purely because I'm not sure you would want to get romantically involved with someone who was so negative! Also, remember to make sure you don't use language like this about yourself!

Some statements are generalizations about how the world is, for example:

❤   'All the good men are taken.'
❤   'Men are unfaithful.'

Here, if you want to pull this person out of their limiting world, you can ask things like:

♥ 'What, you mean there are absolutely no good men left in the world at all, not even one?'

♥ 'Are you saying that there's not one man in the whole wide world who is capable of fidelity? Surely not?'

Clarifying Meaning

Sometimes people aren't generalizing, but using words that have a specific meaning for them – one that you might not share. For example, if someone said to you, 'I want you to be more romantic,' wouldn't it be useful to have a little more information about what being romantic means to them?

You'd get a lot more information if you asked: *'How do you want me to be more romantic?'* or *'What would you like me to do or say that would be romantic?'*

Be careful how much you try to unpick, though. Taking this to its logical conclusion you could ask, 'More romantic than what?' and that would be very irritating!

Rules

People also use statements to create 'rules' about how the world will be, for example, 'It's obvious she won't fancy me.'

Challenge this by asking, *'To whom is it obvious?'*

'Verbalizing'

One that is very common is: 'My relationship isn't going well.' Here we are taking a verb and turning it into a noun. In order to unpick the meaning of this you have to get back the verb. So, in this case you can ask, *'In what way are you not relating well?'*

Limitations

Some people put limitations on themselves, for example: 'I can't dance in front of other people' or 'I just couldn't say "no".'

If you want to encourage them to see more opportunities, you can ask questions like: *'What would happen if you did?'*

Some limitations are based on other people's rules, or rules that you have adopted without checking whether they are useful, for example:

- ❤ 'I must consider my reputation.'
- ❤ 'Girls shouldn't make the first move.'
- ❤ 'I should call her every day.'

Do you make statements like this? I invite you to ask yourself where these rules came from and how useful they are to you. When you hear yourself using words like 'should', 'must', 'can't', oughtn't', 'shouldn't', 'ought to' and 'mustn't', ask yourself: *'What would happen if . . .?'* For example:

- ❤ 'What would happen if I didn't consider my reputation?'
- ❤ 'What would happen if I did make the first move?'
- ❤ 'What would happen if I didn't?'

And, if you feel so inclined and it's useful for the furtherance of your interaction with someone else, you can ask them the questions too. This is a useful tool for gaining perspective on a situation that sometimes seems finite!

Cause and Effect

Some statements are assuming a cause for someone's action, for example, 'You don't bring me flowers – you don't love me' and 'He calls me every day – he must be desperate.'

Here you can ask:

- ❤ 'How does not bringing flowers mean that I don't love you?'
- ❤ 'How does him calling every day make him desperate? Are there other reasons why he might call every day – like he loves talking to you?!'

Mind Reading

Linked to this is mind reading, as in 'He hates me' or 'If you loved me you'd know how to please me.' These statements are pure mind reading. And the purest challenge you can make to this is: *'How do you know?'*

By challenging a person in this way, you are prompting them to come up with evidence – and think about the reality of the statement.

Giving Away Personal Responsibility

These kind of statements are bred from a victim-like status, for example:

- 'You made me angry.'
- 'Whenever you don't call me, I feel bad.'
- 'I wish she wouldn't nag me, I feel so useless.'

When you hear yourself or others making this kind of statement, stop and think: 'Am I giving away responsibility for my feelings? Do other people have power over me?'

You could ask yourself: *'What am I doing to perpetrate victim status here?'*

WORK IT OUT FOR YOURSELF

Every day you will hear people using these language patterns. As you listen to others, consider:

- In which statements is information missing that might lead to confusion?
- In which statements are there massive generalizations about the world?
- Which statements are limiting the opening out of possibilities?
- Which statements are indicative of imposed rules of behaviour?
- Which statements are creating solid meaning from flimsy evidence?
- Which statements are giving away responsibility for feelings to an outside party?
- Which statements are making presumptions about what someone else is thinking or feeling?

This will prompt you to clarify meaning and avoid jumping to conclusions. If you wish, when you notice these language patterns, you can use the appropriate questions to turn that person around.

COLUMBO'S OPENING MOVE

Sometimes it helps to develop a friendly way of asking questions without coming across as a paid-up member of the Spanish Inquisition.

If you have seen *Columbo* on TV, you will be familiar with the way the detective looks confused, scratches his head, tilts it to one side and says in that innocent kind of way, 'Now let me just get this clear. I'm a bit slow and need to go back over what you said.'

You can develop your own Columbo-like clarification openers:

❤ 'I'm sorry, I'm a little confused. Can I check, did you just say. . .?'
❤ 'Gosh, that sounds interesting, but there are a couple of things I'm not sure I got properly. Could you bear with me and clarify. . .?'

Creating 'Columbo' opening statements allows you to challenge what people say without sounding like a cross-examining lawyer.

WHY? THE WORST QUESTION IN THE WORLD

❤ Why do you always forget what I tell you?
❤ Why did you do that?
❤ Why did she reject me?
❤ *Why* do we use this word so much and what effect does it have?

When you ask *'Why?'*, especially in relation to unproductive actions, you immediately send either yourself or another person on an unconscious search for *justification*. And when the word is used accusingly or with negative emphasis, people sometimes find themselves giving self-deprecating answers:

'Why do you always forget my birthday?'
'Because you forget things that are important to me.'
'Because I'm thoughtless, have a bad memory, etc. . .'

Sometimes, instead of a self-deprecating answer you might push someone to come out with a stream of negatives about you, especially if you ask in an accusing way, as is often the case when 'why' comes into play. Be careful about using 'why', because it can put people on the defensive and they may answer back with words which they don't necessarily mean and which can be hurtful to you.

WHAT'S BETTER THAN WHY?

So, what alternatives are there?

Imagine you have just approached someone and been rejected. Instead of saying, 'Why did I make such a mess of that?', you could ask yourself:

- 💜 'How could I avoid that next time?'
- 💜 'How can I change my behaviour to make the next time turn out better?'
- 💜 'What can I learn from the rejection that will improve my chances?'
- 💜 'In what way can I change what I need to in order to be more [whatever the opposite is of the negative word you want to use]?'

These alternative questions will lead to more positive and useful answers which in turn will lead to more positive and useful actions. You will be seen as a more positive and useful person! And people will enjoy being with you. And who knows where that will lead?

TALKING TO YOURSELF

WORDS LEAD TO EMOTIONS

I was reading an e-mail from a friend and was struck by the number of negative words she had used. Every other word was 'depressed' or 'annoyed'. What do you think was happening to her as she wrote those words? Words, as you know, incite emotions. By the end of the e-mail, she must have been feeling even more depressed and annoyed!

Remember that people are attracted to sunshiners. Your words can mark you out as a black-clouder or a sunshiner. Which do you want to be?

Which words do you use on a regular basis that might not be so useful? Which words could you use instead?

One of the most limiting words we use is 'problem'. Do you use this word indiscriminately? I used to use it all the time! Now I have set a trigger for certain 'negative' words I used to use so that when they come to mind, I automatically think of an alternative 'new possibility' word.

NEW POSSIBILITY WORDS

- ♥ Think of a situation or a potential situation that you label a 'problem'. How does it make you feel? Notice what is going on in your body, what images, sounds and feelings you are getting.
- ♥ Now think of that same situation as a 'challenge'. How does that change the way you feel? Does the idea of something being a challenge open out more possibilities? Of course it does!
- ♥ Make a list of three limiting and emotionally negative words that you use on a regular basis.
- ♥ Look at those words and come up with some alternative 'new possibility' words.
- ♥ As you do so, check how these new possibility words make you feel compared to the old limiting words.

When you start to use words that are linked to possibility rather than impossibility, you create more openings for yourself. Unconsciously, you will start to give off different signals and others will pick up on this. The opportunities available to you will automatically increase as more of the right people are drawn to your sunshiney character.

A FINAL WORD

There are many ways in which you can use language to influence people and there are many methods of gaining clarity and insight into what someone is saying. As you begin to pay attention to language, you will hear more and more of these patterns and notice how they pepper our everyday speech.

I invite you to work on learning these patterns and how they can be used for positive rather than negative effect. Write out as many of the persuasive patterns as you need to and begin to use them.

When you hear statements that generalize, delete or distort information, practise in your head any verbal challenges you might want to make. When you feel comfortable doing this and when it is important to the furtherance of a positive interaction between you and another person, you can gently begin to challenge their inhibitory or vague statements out loud.

Try it out with your friends first and notice their reactions. Remember to be alert and sharpen up your senses because people will demonstrate their reactions in their body as well as their words.

I know you are going to use these powerful patterns wisely to make people feel good and communicate as a luscious linguist!

INTEGRATION *part three*

YOUR FLIRTATIOUS *future*

THE ADVENTURE OF YOUR LIFE

You can never set sail for new oceans until you lose sight of the shore.

Now that you have learned a whole load of attitudes and ways of thinking about yourself, as well as some great skills, how do you take the new flirtatious you into the future and really begin to flirt for what you want?

LISTEN TO YOURSELF

You are on the adventure of your life. Out there wonderful things are waiting for you. Listen to your own messages. Answer the calls that are coming from who you really are!

Ask yourself:

❤ Do I hear something calling me?
❤ Am I resisting something that may be a call?

- Is it temptingly juicy?
- What's stopping me?
- What will happen if I don't do this?
- What will happen if I do this?

Remember he who hesitates . . . waits and waits and waits.

THE KEYS TO MAKING IT HAPPEN

When you know what you want, you can begin to dream it. People who are good at manifesting their dreams have several things in common. Here are the key points that will help you become successful in this way. You have to:

- know how you want your life to be
- have a powerful vision of it
- regularly spend time living out this vision in your head
- believe in yourself, take risks and go for it
- know that connecting to others is vital for your success

WHAT DO YOU WANT *NOW*?

The capacity for hope is the most significant fact of life. It provides human beings with a sense of destination and the energy to get started.

Norman Cousins

SAMMI'S STORY:
Making It Happen

My friend Susan's son Sammi has this wonderful ability to get what he wants. He thinks about it and acts *as if* it is happening. He says to himself, 'I'm going to get this.' It usually works. But when he doesn't get something, he just says, 'Oh well, perhaps that wasn't meant to be *yet*!' Sammi is 10!

When people think big, 'create intents' for how they want their life to be and believe it, they begin to move in the right direction.

Great things are only possible with outrageous requests.

Thea Alexander

YOUR INTENT

When you are standing in your sliver of space being your best you, absolutely, that's when you will be magnificent and wonderful and truly flirtatious in the spirit of this book.

Access that sense of who you are and how you are at your best and from there begin to think about your connection to the world. It is in the link between who you are and the world outside that you will discover your intent.

Intent is the great plan you have for your life in relation to the world and yourself. It is not so much a detailed scheme as a sense of how you want to be. It is a direction in which to be going. In my life I have an intent to open doors to people to allow them to grow as I grow myself. I have beliefs that guide me and I trust that whatever happens does so for a reason and that when I give out and connect, I get back what I need. And if I don't get back what I think I need, it is for me to learn why and change!

Creating your intent is not about setting goals for your future, it is about having in mind a sense of how it should be and being able to gauge each action you take against that by asking: 'Does this fit my intent? Is this going to take me closer to how I want to be?'

What has this got to do with flirting? Flirting is a connection with others, and in order to make that connection in the purest and most successful way you have to feel good about yourself and have a sense of what you want to be doing.

When you consider how you want your life to be, it is useful to be aware of certain ways of thinking that will hinder you. Here are a few examples.

- 💜 *'I want to be younger.'* Don't! You cannot turn back time. However, you could wish to live life with a younger attitude and have the enthusiasm and excitement of your youth – that's very different *and* it's attainable.

- 💜 *'I want to be more beautiful.'* Discard this if it is about physical features. You are a unique beautiful individual and whilst you cannot change the outside casing of your body, you *can* change and polish what is inside. Beauty is not about physical features, but about how much of your inner beauty you give out to the world.

- 💜 *'I want to win the lottery.'* Living to win the lottery is giving all control to Fate. Ask yourself what winning the lottery would get you. As long as you come up with material goods, ask the question 'And what will *that* get me?' until you come up with some great sense of how you want to be. You will know it when you get there, because it usually has some connection to words like 'freedom', 'contentment', 'success', 'bliss' or 'happiness'. Make that your intent and work back from there finding ways to be content, blissful and happy that don't require you to win games of chance!

- 💜 *'I want to find my other half.'* Another person will not make you whole and if you think it will, you are asking for trouble. If you want a successful relationship, wish to be the kind of person who is whole and happy enough to attract Mr or Ms Right. See another person as someone who you are with because they enhance your wholeness, not help to create it.

Now look at each of the categories below and allow yourself to dream. Just choose those that are important to you. You don't have to do them all if you don't want to.

As you begin to dream, write down what comes into your head. Let it flow. Don't get too specific. Make this a big picture, a powerful dream – one that you're going to love living!

CATEGORY	WHAT DO YOU WANT?
Love/Romance	
Friendships	
Career	

As you look over your answers, ask yourself how *you* would have to be in order to achieve this. For example, if you want a specific kind of love or relationship how would you have to be in order to attract such a relationship?

A JOURNEY INTO YOUR FUTURE

I want you to be ahead of the 'now' so that you can see what's coming.

Richard Bandler

This exploration involves 'acting out' a walk into the future. In order to do this, find a place where you can move along a length of about 10 feet. Outdoors is great, of course. Just make sure you aren't disturbed.

- Stand on a spot that allows you to move forward in a line a maximum of 10 feet.
- Mark out that spot in your mind or with a piece of paper as the 'now' spot.
- Stand in the 'now' spot and look ahead of you. Imagine that your future is ahead of you.
- Think about a dream that you want to have come true from one of the categories.
- Mark out in your mind a spot on the imaginary line that can represent this event in time. This is your 'dream come true' spot.
- Look at that spot and think of yourself at your best or as your animal or whatever you need to do to feel good about yourself.
- Imagine your future dream is drawing you towards it. Feel it, see it and hear it.

- Step forwards slowly until you arrive at your future dream.
- Stand on this spot and get into the experience of what you are doing in the future, as if it were happening in real time. Make sure that you are seeing it through your own eyes, add in colour and make it a life-size movie. Hear the sounds you'd hear that make you feel good. Juice it up, breathe into it. Spend as long as you need until it feels right and excitingly compelling. Get a sense of it until it feels right. Check this feeling against the feeling of being at your best and against times when things have gone just as you wished and you felt as if you were doing 'you'. You will know when it feels right.
- Step a little further as if moving forward in time. This spot is the 'future future'.
- Turn around and look back at the spot that represented the dream come true time.
- From here in the 'future future', with the ability to look back and see something after it's done, what do you know about how you made your dreams come true? What message would you send yourself? Say it out loud. It is accurate because you are creating it and what you create in your mind now becomes something that you are drawn to and you begin to act as if it is going to happen and somehow things seem to come together to make it happen. If it doesn't, it is because you need to learn something before you get it.
- And then move back into the 'dream come true' place. Get into it again. And from there turn back and look at the 'now' spot.
- What is it like living this dream? How did it happen? What message would you send yourself? Say it out loud.
- Return to the 'now' spot. Imagine you can see yourself at the 'dreams come true' spot and ask yourself what you have learnt about the future and how to make it happen the way you want. Say it out loud.
- When you are ready, sit down and write out the lessons you learned from this experience.

FLIRT COACH

GO ON, SELL YOURSELF!

Remember how at the beginning of this book I asked you what kind of person you were? I am sure that by now you have discovered a great deal about your unique talents and abilities. If you had to write an advert that would convey all those qualities and get across the kind of person you really are, what would you write?

YOUR ADVERTISEMENT

Just sit for a moment and imagine yourself at your best, capable of making dreams come true, flirtatiously successful in every way. Write an ad to promote yourself at your best:

When you choose me, you will be with a person who. . .

And when someone significant enters your life, always ask yourself, are you more or less of who you are when you are with them?

Now that you know how to create a sense of your dream future, how do you go about making it happen? One of the most important keys to getting what you want is to realize the power of connecting with other people.

THE POWER OF CONNECTING

How many people do you know? Who are they? What links do they have? What made you connect with them? How do you get to someone you need to get to? How do you find old friends? How do you get financial backing? How do you get those jobs that are never advertised? How do you get to meet the one for you? Simple! You connect with as many people as possible and ask!

Here are some real-life examples of how connecting gets results in all areas.

Finding a Home

When I was looking for somewhere to live, I sent an e-mail to a list of 700 people. I received the offer of a cottage in the countryside, a large self-contained attic above a friend's house, a share of a house on the edge of the water and a houseboat. I wouldn't have found any of those through normal channels.

Finding Financial Backing

Jeff Cain asked and asked. The last major connection he made was finding backers to start his chatline business. Jeff connected his way to success. You can do it too, as did some of the participants on my flirting weekend.

Finding a Partner

Paul met Adrian on a flirting weekend. They went out and practised their skills together. At one social event, Paul met Adrian's ex-girlfriend and they fell in love.

Marie decided to join a dating agency. Before she had always thought these places were for desperate people. By taking the risk and connecting, she discovered the truth – dating agencies are great places to meet a partner. Marie did. So, get connected and sign up!

Making Wonderful Friends

I've hung out on various forums and lists on the Internet for years. After sussing out a list, I start to ask questions like:

- ❤ What do you think about X?
- ❤ How can I find Y?

I get lots of replies and in this way have connected with some powerful people in my field. These friendships have blossomed online and now that I have met many of these people in the flesh as well, virtual friendships have become real friendships *and* business opportunities – and is there a difference, I wonder? These friendships have also generated untold extra connections.

Some connections can have direct results, while others lead to more connections. You never know until you make them!

THE SIX DEGREES OF CONNECTION

Are you familiar with the six degrees of separation theory? In the late '60s, the psychologist Stanley Milgram ran an experiment to find out the answer to the question: 'Are all human beings connected?' From his research, Milgram deduced that:

You are within six links of connecting to anyone you need to meet.

I like to think of this as the six degrees of connection.

Malcolm Gladwell, author of *The Tipping Point*, has expanded on Milgram's theory. Gladwell reckons that in every community there are a few people who have very extensive connections. It is only when you are one of these people or directly connected to one that the six-degree effect works. Gladwell calls these people Connectors. The good news is that all of us know or have the potential to know someone who is a Connector.

This theory works for me because it matches the evidence of my own life. And we do tend to believe the evidence of our own experiences and that of likeminded people around us, don't we?

Sprinkled among every walk of life . . . are a handful of people with a truly extraordinary knack of making friends and acquaintances.
Malcolm Gladwell

Do you know a Connector? Are you a Connector? Can you become one? What possibilities could it open out to you?

WHAT DOES IT TAKE TO BE A CONNECTOR?

What do Connectors have in common? Here's what I found by asking my Connector friends:

- ♥ They feel good about themselves.
- ♥ They absolutely love people.
- ♥ They love socializing.

- ❤ They are always curious about other people.
- ❤ They are aware of the powerful benefits of connecting.
- ❤ They ask for help and they offer help.
- ❤ They love facilitating connections between people they are connected to.

PRACTICAL TIPS FOR POTENTIAL CONNECTORS

Here are a few hints on how to develop your connectability.

POLISH YOUR CONNECTOR MUSCLES

In order to connect successfully you have to get into Connector mode. The following workout will help you.

A GENTLE CONNECTING WORKOUT

- ❤ Always start by getting into how you are at your best.
- ❤ Spend at least 10 minutes a day thinking positive thoughts about someone you don't connect well with.
- ❤ Spend at least 10 minutes a day thinking about all the things you like about someone you know. Then tell them.
- ❤ Spend time imagining the world as a sandpit and all the people as fellow children playing with you.
- ❤ Spend five minutes every day affirming that you will make a new connection today, no matter how small.
- ❤ Think of everyone you meet as a special person who has some surprisingly endearing qualities that you can discover if you wish.
- ❤ When you have to go to a social function think, 'I wonder who is going to cross my path tonight and what it will signify?'
- ❤ If someone catches your eye and you get a feeling about them, follow it up.
- ❤ If you meet someone and want to follow up the connection, ask them for a card. Give them your card in return. You obviously have a good reason for wanting to know them. If it's genuine they will appreciate it and feel good.

- Have separate business and personal cards. The card you give sends the right message from the start.
- When you have a moment, write on the back of someone's card any notes that will remind you of them.
- If you get invited to parties where you don't know anyone or have to travel alone, see it as an opportunity to meet new people.
- Think of all the places you can make more connections and all the places where you haven't made any yet, but can.
- Consider that each challenge you face is an opportunity to connect by reaching out and asking for help.

YOU ARE PART OF A NETWORK OF CONNECTIONS

You are already connected to many people. A great way to realize this is to physically map out the connections you already have. You will be surprised at how well connected you are!

MAPPING OUT YOUR NETWORK

You will need a big piece of paper – flip-chart size or larger. In the middle draw a symbol that represents you.

- Start drawing lines outwards from this symbol like rays streaming out from the sun. Make enough space in between the lines so that you can write on each one.
- Begin to think of all the connections you have and as names come up, put one on each line. Some ideas to get you going: schoolfriends, neighbourhood friends, family, work colleagues, out-of-work colleagues, shopkeepers, Internet friends, fellow group members, fellow hobbyists, people in bars you visit, religious groups, people who have given you dust-covered business cards. . .
- When you have mapped out a lot of direct connections, go back and look at each one with these thoughts in mind:

Who do they know?

What do I associate with them?

💜 The best way to do this is to relax and allow the connections to emerge. Go with what comes up.

💜 Keep adding to this map as you meet new people. Eventually you might even have to get a computer program to deal with the ever-expanding content of your network!

💜 When you think about your dreams for the future, look back at your map and let ideas click in.

Do this often and do it with a sense of excitement. Think of all the different people you encounter in your daily life and haven't yet connected with. Where could a chance connection lead you? Who knows what knowledge, information, leads, friends, connections, affiliations, power, commonalities you might link up to when you plug into the grid?

SETTING OFF YOUR OWN CHAIN REACTION

If you want to reach someone or need something, you can, via your connections, set off a chain of enquiry that will bring results. Start by thinking of a person who might know someone. It's easy when you've mapped it out.

If you don't ask, you don't get. Most people love to help, sometimes more than they love to *be* helped! As long as your intentions are positive and honourable, it's OK to ask. And eventually you will discover that what goes around really does come around. It's a two-way street!

WHAT CONNECTIONS DO YOU NEED TO MAKE RIGHT NOW?

💜 Think of that great big dream of how you want your life to be.

💜 How can connecting help to realize this dream? Ask yourself which of your connections is most likely to get you closer to what you want. Write down the names.

- As you look at all the names, consider who they might know.
- Ask what skills they have that can help you.
- Ask what information they have that can help you.
- Think of someone you'd like to connect with but don't know how to.
- Start with your network and consider who is most likely to lead you in the right direction.
- Consider all the people you are connected to. Who are they are connected to. . .
- Connect with someone now!

If you have a dream in mind, the more people you share it with, the greater your chances of making it happen.

Once you connect with someone, make sure you always ask for an e-mail address before you take a phone number. E-mail is a quick and non-intrusive way of keeping in touch. Always volunteer your details too. If you don't have e-mail yet, get connected now!

Within a week of meeting the person, you should make a quick call or, better still, send a short e-mail to say how nice it was to meet them. This activates the connection.

Once connected, you are in that person's mental or other database and they in yours, waiting to pop up at the right time.

RECONNECTING

When we met in London in the '80s, Ali and I had some fun times together. We lost touch but I found him by searching the Internet. He was living in New York and I spent time with him and his girlfriend when I visited New York. Now I am connected to her, too, and everyone they know. And they are connected to me. And who knows when that connection will serve any or all of us in the future?

- Are there people you want to reconnect with?
- What might they be doing now?
- Where can you start looking?

LOVE CONNECTIONS

Throw your dream into space like a kite, and you do not know what it will bring back –
a new life, a new friend, a new love, or a new country.

Anaïs Nin

I know so many people who have met a partner through joining a dating agency
or a social group or an Internet site or forum. When you join these agencies you
are plugging into the grid of available like-minded people out there. What
opportunities might pass you by if you don't plug in!

I salute everyone who is wise and brave enough to take action, change their
life and start connecting.

Time to get off your backside and go out and take action for yourself!

You can find agencies that specialize in your kind of interests. One dating
agency I know is for non-smokers who are interested in ecology, vegetarianism,
spirituality and other linked activities. They have a great success rate because
they connect like-minded people.

Some companies run 'speed-dating' type events where you get to spend
eight minutes with several people and everyone gets to say whom they want to
meet again. If there's a match, they put you in touch!

There are some great things going on out there. Remember Marie? She got
the courage to connect and met her man. You can too!

ALISON'S STORY:
Must Find a Boyfriend

Alison wanted to find a man. She got together with a group of girlfriends and
formed ABFAB, ABsolutely must Find A Boyfriend. They met once a week,
drank pink champagne and did all kinds of exercises to increase their positivity
and possibilities. They had lots of fun, expanded their social network and one
girl even met her fiancé through another member of the group!

NETTING A PARTNER

The Internet is a great place to meet people. There are hundreds of forums and
dating sites and meeting-places out there for singles.

You can also meet people through your interests. I know a married couple who met on the *Star Trek* site. Shared interests are important in a relationship!

I've spent time on singles sites on the Internet, checking them out. It's perfectly safe if you follow the basic rules of safety and use your senses!

Why stop at your own country, when you could connect with someone abroad? Think wide and go for it!

ATTEND PERSONAL DEVELOPMENT WORKSHOPS

Seminars are great places for meeting people. The best thing of all is that workshops often include lots of interactive explorations and games, so there is a natural mechanism for approaching anyone. What a great way to meet lots of like-minded people in a short space of time!

CAREER AND SOCIAL CONNECTIONS

Whether you are building a career, starting a new business, looking for friends or in search of romance, it is all out there. You just have to start connecting.

PETA'S STORY: *Circular Connections*

I met Mark on an Internet forum. I put something out and he responded. We corresponded over a couple of years.

I quit my job to go freelance and didn't have a lot of work lined up. I didn't realize it then, but I had been unconsciously setting up a web of connections that were to bear juicy fruit.

Three days after my last day as a wage slave, Mark sent me an e-mail. Was I interested in some work with a major German motor manufacturer in sales training? Was I ever!

Recently I had the opportunity to recommend Mark to a friend of mine for some work. And so the world turns!

Connections make the world go round and add to the possibilities of your world!

CREATING SUCCESS CONNECTIONS

Here are some of the things you can set in motion when you connect with a new person. You can:

- connect them to someone else for mutual benefit
- ask them for a specific introduction
- develop a friendship or business relationship
- store their details for future connections
- put them on your personal mailing list

So many people waste time saying, 'Wouldn't it be a good idea if someone arranged this or organized that?' Do you wait for things to happen or do you make them happen? Do you want to achieve something but feel you need help? Would you like to have a team of supporters cheering you on?

You can create your own success group to offer mutual support for individual projects and dreams in a practical way.

STARTING YOUR OWN SUCCESS GROUP

Here are a few ideas on how to begin:

- Decide what kind of people you want in your group.
- Advertise, speak out at a meeting, ask people.
- Keep your group small – six to eight people is a great group size.
- Set up regular meetings.
- Give everyone time to ask for help for specific projects or realizing dreams.
- Use e-mail as an additional resource.

You'll be surprised at how much help you can generate and you'll enjoy being able to help others realize their dreams.

SUSAN'S STORY: *Creating a Group*

My friend Susan, who is into spiritual development, wanted to meet like-minded people. She put an advertisement in the local paper. Thirty people responded and soon she had a group meeting at her home every week. From running this small group Susan graduated to putting on her own workshops.

By taking that first step Susan has enriched her circle of friends and her career and life in general. What easy first step could you take?

A FINAL WORD

Now is the time for you to set free your flirtatious self and really go for what you want. There is a whole world out there waiting to help you fulfil those great big dreams. You have the abilities, you can develop the skills if you do the work and you will find your world changing as you put in the effort to make it happen! This is true SuccessFlirting!

Thank you for taking the time to read this book. My one hope is that somewhere, somehow, something has made you sit up and take notice and if there is just one thing that resonated with you, then I've done my job. I encourage you to continue to learn and read and look for ways to develop yourself personally. You only have one life and it is happening now. Remember to be how you are at your best at all times and go out there and flirt for whatever you want *right now*!

And, you can begin right now to exercise your flirt muscle by trying out the '30 ways to a more flirtatious you. . .'

THIRTY WAYS TO
a more flirtatious you

Be nice to yourself and explore at least one of the suggestions below every day.
Try new ones out on a daily basis.

Make as much time as you need to integrate these ideas easily and
comfortably. Fifteen minutes a day is a minimum. Many of these suggestions
can be done while you are showering, travelling to work or just walking around
or during any idle moment.

1   *Positively great surroundings*
    Seek out sunshiners and stay away from black-clouders. Surround yourself with
    things that make you feel good, like quotes and pictures that motivate you and
    generate good feelings. Post them on your walls, or on your screensaver if you
    have a computer, and if you don't yet have an online connection, get one. . .

2   *Laughter, the best medicine*
    Are you laughing enough? Find things that make you laugh. Watch TV
    programmes that make you laugh. Read books that make you laugh. Do things
    that make you laugh. Connect and spend time with people that make you laugh.
    Subscribe to a daily joke list.

3   *Mirror, mirror. . .*

Whenever you stand in front of the mirror ask yourself: 'What's true of me when I am at my best, absolutely? What am I like when I'm [use the word you found to represent yourself at your best *(see p.54)*]? How am I at my best when I am being [and use your word for this] wonderful and totally myself?'

4   *Awaken in Paradise*

When you wake up in the morning, find time to answer the Wake Up in Paradise questions *(see page 82)*. You can do them anywhere by just asking them in your head.

5   *A bountiful day*

Each day as you wake up, ask: 'What wonders await me today?' If life gets tough at any point during the day, ask: 'What's happening here? What have I got to learn? What next?'

6   *Five-dimensional sensing*

As you go about your business, take in the world through each individual sense. Notice the different information that becomes available to you.

7   *The animal knows*

If you found an animal symbol or totem, spend time getting to know what your animal is like and discovering which of its qualities you need. What might your animal be telling you? Take time to shift into the animal *(see page 57)* and sense the world like that.

8   *Spicy variety*

Decide that each day you will do something in a different way. Take another route to work, change the order of your routine. Turn off the TV for a night and read. Walk at a different pace. Variety, as they say, is the spice of life. And it's true!

9   *'Diarize' it*

Keep a journal. Spend five minutes or so just before you go to bed reviewing the day and writing down whatever comes to mind. 'Diarizing' your thoughts will open you up to recognition of what you have learned and to new ideas.

10 *It is a great day*

At the end of each day ask yourself: 'What great things happened today?' This will focus you on the positive as an antidote to the negative things we sometimes seem to prioritize.

11 *Dream up the answers*

Before you go to sleep, ask yourself a question for which you sense you need an answer. It can be about anything in your life. Should I call that person? What's my next career move? Just ask yourself gently the moment before you drift off into sleep and be prepared to awake in the morning with more clarity.

12 *The natural way to go*

Here's a simple way to get five minutes of peace. Stand somewhere in nature, even if it's a small patch of grass. Let your body relax slowly as you breathe and just sense the earth renewing you. Feel as though you are breathing in through your left foot and out through your right foot. Let all the problems and cares of the day sink out into the earth. Continue doing this looping breathing. It's very peace inducing.

13 *The gift of your smile*

Start smiling at strangers. As you see people coming towards you, focus on them and think of how good you feel, and as they get closer, smile and say 'Hi' if you wish. (Avoid doing this in lonely places or late at night!)

14 *The freedom of dancing*

Learn to dance a wild dance. It can be hula or ceroq or merengue, salsa, tango – anything, as long as it gets you to move and sway in a sexy way. Join a class, check out the local directories, hire or buy a video, mimic dancing on TV! It will open you up and you meet people at dancing classes!

15 *Check your voice*

If your voice needs work, do the voice work exercises *(see pages 95–100)* and start to look for voice therapists. If you don't know where to start, ask five people. Someone will have the answer!

16 *Feed your passion*

Join a group that feeds your passion. If there isn't one, start one. Put an advert in the local newspaper and state what you want. People will respond.

17 *You are a sexual being*

Spend time enjoying your sexuality. Set aside time once a week to indulge yourself sexually and explore ways in which your body can experience more pleasure.

18 *Get connected*

Spend time connecting. Go to exhibitions and conferences and groups and learn and have fun. Take cards with you. Approach strangers wantonly. In some of these places, you are all there with a common bond – it's a chance to connect.

19 *Daydream your future*

Spend time daydreaming. You can allocate time to it every day. Sit down quietly and as you relax, think of the life you want. Do the 'Journey into your Future' exercise *(see page 191)* and practise living your future. This gets it into your body more and makes it a reality to your brain.

20 *The world is your playpen*

When you are in groups of people, take a few minutes to become an observer. Begin to notice the words the people use, their phrases, their rhythm, their movements. Beware of judgements and labels. Just notice that they use certain words and move in certain ways. This sharpens up your senses and gives you material to work with.

21 *It's elemental – movement, that is*

To hone your flexibility, spend time moving in different elements. Try walking around in a fiery way, or an airy way, or a slinky flowing way or a solid rooted way. You will be surprised how much this helps you when you are approaching strangers.

22 *Secret agent of signals*

When you are in social arenas, become an observer, a secret agent of signals. Watch what people do and the interactions between them. Try to guess what is going on. Use your senses and your observation skills.

23 *Learn, learn, learn*

Each day promise yourself that you will do something towards learning something new and useful. What have you always wanted to learn? It might be a language, a new skill, a new way of doing something at work, a new phone number, a new sexual position, the choice is yours. . .

24 *Ready to connect*

Have personal cards printed. Make them very representative of you. If you are wary of handing out your home number, use your mobile or pager number. Find a quote that represents you and print it underneath your name. If you want to add business details, feel free to do so. If you can, print them on the back of the card. Leave a space for additional details you might want to add. Be creative.

25 *Am I doing me?*

Take some time to examine the work you do. Is it really you? If it is, great! If not, ask yourself: 'What do I really, really want?' and 'What do I need to do to move?' Get some career counselling or buy a book on the subject. Start working on realizing your true working dream.

26 *Finding your style*

Does your external appearance reflect your true style? Do the colours that you wear suit your skin tone? Is your haircut flattering to your face? Do the clothes you wear reflect you at your best? Are there certain fashions or clothes or jewellery you would like to wear but don't, *yet*? Buy something like that and wear it. Are you hiding certain attributes? Show them off! Find your real style!

27 *Complimentingly great*

Spend time observing people and noting what you like about them. Give out at least one or two compliments a day. If people have been useful, helpful, positive, successful or just smiled, tell them you appreciate it.

28 *Banish black clouds*

Be alert for black-clouders. If you sense for a moment that their cloud is overshadowing you or they are going on a negative downward spiral, use your language skills and rapport skills to lead them elsewhere. If you can't – move on. Avoid negative energy. There are plenty of sunshiners out there.

29 *Love is all around*

If you are looking for love, start researching different avenues. Try dating agencies, the Internet, ask friends. Start a group, give a party and ask all your single friends to bring a single friend of the opposite sex. Put in an advert, go on TV, whatever you haven't tried yet.

30 *Exercise those muscles*

Make sure you go back through the book and do the explorations. Practise them as often as you need to polish up those flirting muscles!

RESOURCES

Learning a skill is like opening a doorway. Though the door can be opened by another, each person must walk through for themselves if they are to attain mastery of that skill.

This section is a personal selection of books, courses, tapes and resources on a number of specialized subjects that are in some way linked to the work I do. Many of these have profoundly affected me during my journey of personal growth.

My hope in offering this range of resources is that something will spark off in you and lead you to continue your own journey in your own way.

HIGHLY RECOMMENDED READING

The books listed below have been major turning-points in my development and my way of thinking. I heartily recommend them.

If you cannot find some of these in your local bookshop, remember that Internet companies like **amazon.com** and **amazon.co.uk** and **Barnes and**

Noble.com can supply almost any book and bookshops are happy to order books provided you have an author and title.

Carol Adrienne, *The Purpose of Your Life*
If you feel that you have a purpose in life that you have not yet discovered or if you feel
   you know your purpose but want to be more certain about it, this book will guide
   you through a process of self-discovery that is truly empowering.

Ted Andrews, *Animal Speak*
I was already an animal lover, but Ted Andrews awakened me to the magic of animals
   and all that they have to teach us. This is a truly magical book filled with many
   useful exercises that expand on the work we did here on animal symbols.

Richard Bandler, *Magic in Action*
This book is a transcript of Richard Bandler doing fabulous changework with clients –
   an inspiration and a great testament to the efficacy of Neuro Linguistic
   Programming.

Richard Bandler and John LaValle, *Persuasion Engineering*, Meta Publications
This has to be my favourite book on the art of persuasion. If you have not heard John
   or Richard speak, you may need to relax as you read and accept that it is very
   hypnotically written. Inside that hypnotic trance are some wonderful gems of deep
   learning on how to help engineer decisions that are right for everyone.

Barefoot Doctor, *Barefoot Doctor's Handbook for the Urban Warrior: A Spiritual Survival
   Guide*
This is one of my all-time favourite books. It is a wonderful collection of exercises for
   awakening your energy. They are easy to do and very powerful. Well written,
   simple and funny.

Richard Brodie, *Virus of the Mind*
If you want to know more about how people are mentally programmed by ideas and
   how to program yourself for more useful beliefs, read this book!

Larry Dossey, *Be Careful What You Pray For – You Might Get It*

Larry Dossey, an American medical doctor, examines the hefty evidence in favour of
the power of thought to hex and to cure. If you are in any way interested in how
belief systems are formed and how powerful your words can be, read this book.
It may save your life or someone else's.

Thom Hartmann, *Last Hours of Ancient Sunlight*

This book moved me profoundly. It is a call to the heart to wake up to what is going on
in the world and a path to adapting the ways of the older cultures to regain what
we risk losing. This book has nothing to do with flirting or romance, but it does
have something to do with the way we are choosing to live our lives and
consideration for others.

Julia Henderson, *The Lover Within*

This is a great little workbook for developing your sexual energy and enhancing your
sexual ecstasy. I recommend it as an easy beginner's guidebook.

Diane K. Osborn (ed.), *Reflections on the Art of Living: A Joseph Campbell Companion*

This book presents the basic philosophy that has influenced my work. It is a treasure
trove of ways of living that allow you to flourish as your true self – a wonderful
book.

John Perkins, *Shapeshifting*

This enchanting account of John Perkins' travels among the indigenous tribes of South
America and Indonesia is a true awakening to the possibilities that lie out there.
Perkins gives an account of shamans' abilities to dream travel and shapeshift into
the spirits of animals. Although this might sound strange, if you have done the
exercises in this book, you have tried some of this already! I also recommend all
John Perkins' other books.

Candace Pert, *Molecules of Emotion*

Candace Pert has proved scientifically that emotion can be formed in cell structures,
that we do indeed form molecules of emotion. This book is a useful reference for

the scientifically minded and an interesting account of a woman's struggle in the male-dominated world of science.

James Redfield, *The Celestine Prophecy*
A global bestseller in which James Redfield has opened out to the general public a world of synchronicity, energy and spiritual discovery. This book is mind-blowing. Read it now!

Tony Robbins, *Awaken the Giant Within*
Tony is a powerful motivational speaker and this book is a positive workout for the enthusiastic. Robbins spares no pain as he drives you on. He gave me motivation, energy and a 'go for it' attitude.

Barbara Sher, *Wishcraft*
This was the first book that really opened me to the possibilities that I can live the life I love and love the life I live. I also recommend all Barbara Sher's other books.

Neale Donald Walsch, *Conversations with God*
In this world-wide bestseller, Walsch echoes the surge of the spiritual sense rising in all of us. He has opened to the world at large the thoughts that many of us have had for years – that there is more out there and there are better ways of living.

OTHER BOOKS
FLIRTING AND RELATIONSHIPS

David M. Buss, *The Evolution of Desire*, Basic Books
An in-depth study of human mating behaviour. Explains a lot!

Helen Fisher, *Anatomy of Love*
A cross-cultural study of marriage, mating, flirting, sex, adultery and more. Very enlightening.

Bradley Gerstman, Christopher Pizzo and Rich Seldes, *What Men Want*, HarperCollins
A fascinating insight into 30-something American male yuppies' ideas of how women should be.

Lillian Glass, *Attracting Terrific People*
Great little workbook for helping uncover your best you.

John Gray, *Mars and Venus on a Date*
Some of my flirting course participants have found this book 'like a clearing of the mists'! It encourages you to consider other perspectives.

Susan Jeffers, *Opening our Hearts to Men*
How to avoid dependency.

Leil Lowndes, *How to Make Anyone Fall in Love with You* and *How to Talk to Anyone*, Thorsons
Great 'how to' books, once you've got the 'state of being' to do the techniques.

Susan Rabin, *How to Attract Anyone, Anywhere, Anytime*
This is full of useful tips and hints on flirting.

Clare Walker, *Socialising for Success*
Clare attended my flirting class. This is a great logically structured book with plenty of exercises on how to improve your social skills.

Sharyn Wolff, *Guerrilla Dating Tactics*
This offers lots of information on dating tactics, though I'm not sure about the warfare analogy!

SEDUCTION AND SEXUALITY

Mantak Chia, *Taoist Secrets of Love: Cultivating Male Sexual Energy*, Aurora Press
How men can go at it for hours and have multiple orgasms!

Mantak Chia and Douglas Abrams Arava, *The Multi-Orgasmic Man*, Thorsons
This is an ideal beginner's book on tantric sex. Give it as a present – it could change
     your sex life forever!

Richard Craze, *Tantric Sexuality: A Beginner's Guide*
I love this book. It's lighthearted and a great simple introduction to the basics of tantric
     sex without too much emphasis on the spiritual side.

Phillip Hodson and Anne Hooper, *How to Make Great Love to a Man* and *How to Make
     Great Love to a Woman*
These books are fantastic. Read them in juicy anticipation of being in a great
     passionate relationship soon!

Anne Hooper, *The Body Electric*
The story of six women in search of an orgasm. The book takes you through six weeks
     of the sexuality group they attend and you, the reader, become the seventh
     member of the group, able to carry out the same homework as the fictional
     characters. Available from most bookshops and via **www.annehooper.com.**

GENERAL PERSONAL DEVELOPMENT

Robin Chandler and Jo Ellen Grzyb, *The Nice Factor*, Simon & Schuster
How to put your needs first and not live a life wanting to be liked by everyone.

Stephen Covey, *The Seven Habits of Highly Effective People*, Simon & Schuster, 1992
A powerful book on living a healthier, better organized, more relaxed life.

Victor Frankl, *Man's Search for Meaning*

This book is inspiring. If you ever feel like giving up, read this, it'll put things in perspective.

Harriet Goldhor Lerner, *The Dance of Anger*, *The Dance of Intimacy* and *The Dance of Deception*

These are totally brilliant self-development books, written for women, but I recommend them to men as well.

Napoleon Hill, *Think and Grow Rich*

A huge success as a book and business, based on the power of belief in self-ability.

Spencer Johnson, *Who Moved my Cheese?: An Amazing Way to Deal with Change in your Work and in your Life*

This book should be compulsory for life's 'victims'.

Joseph O'Connor and John Seymour, *Introducing Neuro Linguistic Programming*

This is the first book I ever read on NLP, the psychology behind much of what you have been learning in this book. A great beginner's book, but if you are interested, it's wiser to take a course!

SPIRITUALITY

Renée Beck and Sydney Barbara Merrick, *The Art of Ritual*

A beautiful book for creating ritual anywhere, anytime.

Sonia Choquette, *Your Heart's Desire*, Piatkus Books

Thom Hartmann, *The Greatest Spiritual Secret of the Century*

A wonderful parable explaining simple spiritual concepts.

Wayne Dyer, *Real Magic*
This is one of my favourite books on practical spirituality and creating a magical life. It
is a wonderfully empowering read.

Carolyn Myss, *Anatomy of the Spirit*
The seven stages of power and healing.

Clarissa Pinkola Estes, *Women who Run with the Wolves*
These tales and legends reach deep into the spirit. First and foremost for women, they
are also for men who want some insight into female spirituality.

John Roger, *Spiritual Warrior: The Art of Spiritual Living* and *Relationships: The Art of
Making Life Work*

Marianne Williamson, *Return to Love* and *A Woman's Worth*
Return to Love is a discourse on spirituality. Read this book and see how many truths
just spring out of the page at you. It's a must for anyone seeking to find peace. If
you aren't religious, substitute 'Universe' or whatever you want for 'God' and
'Holy Spirit'.
A Woman's Worth is great reading for all women, a lovely bedtime companion and will
send you to sleep dreaming of your power as a woman.

ENERGY WORK

Joy Gardner-Gordon, *Color and Crystals: A Journey Through the Chakras*, Crossing
Press, Inc.

Carol Ritberger, *Your Personality, Your Health: Connecting Personality with the Human
Energy System, Chakras and Wellness*, Hay House, Inc.

MEDITATION AND VISUALIZATION

Shakti Gawain, *Creative Visualisation*
Simple and beautiful, this is the best book on visualization that I've ever read!

Dina Glouberman, *Life Choices, Life Changes*
How to develop a personal vision with imagework. Lots of information on how to use
   visualization.

Helen Graham, *Visualisation: An Introductory Guide*
How to use visualization to improve your health and develop your self-awareness and
   creativity.

DOING WHAT YOU LOVE AND LOVING WHAT YOU DO

Richard N. Bolles, *What Colour is Your Parachute?*
This book is fantastic. Updated yearly, it offers lots of resources, mainly American. It's
   great for uncovering what you love doing and are good at doing and how to go
   about starting it.

Barbara Sher, *I Could Do Anything, If Only I Knew What It Was* and *Live the Life You
   Love*
Barbara's books truly inspired me. They are well worth a read if you want to make a big
   change and do something you've always wanted to.

Nick Williams, *The Work We Were Born to Do*
An excellent book which reviews everything in your life to explain why you are where
   you are today – and makes you do some serious thinking about what your life is
   all about.

MOVEMENT AND DANCE

K. Bloom and R. Shreeves, *Moves: A Sourcebook for Body Awareness and Creative
   Movement*, Harwood Academic, Amsterdam, 1988

Lynne Robinson and Gordon Thomson, *Body Control: The Pilates Way*, Boxtree

Debbie Shapiro, *Your Body Speaks Your Mind*
Very interesting book on how emotions are emitted through your body. This is
   especially good for dealing with stress.

LEARNING, BRAIN AND MIND POWER

Tony Buzan, *The Mind Map Book*, BBC Books

This book helped me increase my creativity tenfold.

Carla Hannaford, *Smart Moves: Why Learning Is Not All in Your Head*, Great Ocean
Publishers, Arlington, Virginia, 1995

Al Koran, *Bring Out the Magic of Your Mind*

Great book for enhancing your ability to be more abundant, magical and intuitive.

INFLUENCE, PERSUASION AND LANGUAGE

Robert B. Cialdini, *The Psychology of Persuasion*, Quill

A fabulous book on the structure and background of influence. A must for all interested
in the art of persuasion!

James Lawley and Penny Tompkins, *Metaphors in Mind: Transformation through
Symbolic Modelling*

A fascinating book on how your metaphors and symbols can be used for personal
transformation.

Deborah Tannen, *You Just Don't Understand: Women and Men in Conversation*, Virago,
1992

A discussion of the ways in which women and men use language differently. Useful for
improving male/female conversation.

COURSES THAT HAVE PROFOUNDLY AFFECTED MY LIFE

Joseph Riggio, *The MythoSelf* series

www.appliednlp.com; jsriggio@appliednlp.com; www.appliednlp.com; Tel. +44 (1)
201 512 8772 International; 1 800 405 6555 Toll Free US

This is the course where I opened out and found my sliver of space. It is about finding
the wonder of yourself. Joseph Riggio is my teacher, mentor and friend, and as I
continue to study with him I find myself becoming more and more of who I am.
This is magic. Several participants from my flirting weekends have subsequently
attended Joseph's courses with fantastic results. Courses are held several times a
year in the USA and the UK. I recommend this man as the most powerful
influence on my life, which is why he is top of my list. Do this course if you want to
find very powerful personal awareness. Highly recommended.

McKenna Breen NLP Practitioner Course

McKenna Breen Limited; **www.mckenna-breen.com;** Tel. +44 (0)20 7704 6604

This is the only UK NLP Practitioner course featuring the originator of NLP, Richard
Bandler, one of my greatest teachers. It is seven days of learning and *fun*. Many
people from my flirting classes have attended this course to expand on and
enhance what they have learnt from me.

Insight – Opening the Heart

Insight Seminars, 37 Spring Street, London W2 1JA; Tel. +44 (0)20 7706 2021

If you have unhealed relationships or are inclined to be a bit of a victim, this course
offers a safe place to really become aware of limiting behaviour and begin the
healing. A good beginner's personal development course. Also available in
America, Australia and many other parts of the world.

OTHER COURSES

FLIRTING AND SEDUCTION

Ross Jeffries, *Basic Speed Seduction Home Study Course* and *How to Have*
Unstoppable Confidence and Power with Women
Straightforward Productions; order from Ross's website, **www.seduction.com**, or
direct from Straightforward Productions, Tel. +1 703 791 6421

All men can benefit from Ross's techniques and women should be aware of them too.
Highly recommended by many of my flirting class graduates.

GENERAL PERSONAL DEVELOPMENT

Outlook Training Seminars
outlooktrg@aol.com, Tel. +44 (0)20 8905 5014

An extremely powerful and enlightening personal development training in which you
access and experience your particular essence, which is unbelievably
empowering.

AUDIO AND VIDEO

VOICE, MUSIC AND MOVEMENT

Products by Dr Morton Cooper, leading US voice expert:
Change your Voice, Change your Life (book)
Winning with your Voice (book)
How to Improve your Speaking Voice (tape)
How to Get a Better More Effective Voice/Breathe Easy, Breathe Right (video)

Most of Dr Cooper's products are obtainable via **amazon.co.uk** and Dr Cooper can be
contacted on the internet on **VOICEDOCTR@aol.com**.

Jonathan Altfeld, *Finding your Irresistible Voice* (2 CD set)
Available from **www.altfeld.com.**

Jonathan's tape will really help you improve that flirtatious voice.

CDS AND TAPES
Kenrick Cleveland, *MaxPersuasion 2000*

Cleveland is a master of persuasion and this is a really good CD series. Obtainable
from **www.maxpersuasion.com**.

Gabrielle Roth and Luna, *The Wave*, Raven Recording, New Bank, New Jersey

Amazingly powerful movement meditation. I use it daily. Very sensual, very powerful,
very liberating.

INTERNET RESOURCES
FLIRTING AND SEDUCTION

cliff@costech.com
A private Internet list on seduction. Open to all to join. Men share their experiences and
successful seduction techniques.
www.fastseduction.com
Website of the alt.seduction.fast newsgroup – lots of stuff on seduction, mainly from
men, but women can learn masses from these groups too.

PETA HESKELL AND THE FLIRTING ACADEMY
www.flirtcoach.com; www.flirtingacademy.com
Check out my constantly updated website which is packed full of articles on a variety
of subjects – tips, solutions to problems, e-mail newsletter access, success
stories, sexual humour, workshop details and links to flirting, sexuality and
personal development sites, plus all the latest news.

I can be contacted via this e-mail number. Please feel free to write to me with any
comments or questions about this book. I will do my best to ensure all electronic
correspondence receives a reply.

info@flirtcoach.com

Tel. +44 (0) 700 4 354 784; e-mail **corporate@flirtcoach.com**

Peta Heskell also offers corporate charisma courses, after-dinner speeches and one-
to-one coaching.

REMEMBER

'Live the life you love and love the life you live to find yourelf loving someone, loving
you, loving yourself.'